1981

SIGNIFICANT DECISIONS OF THE SUPREME COURT, 1976-1977 TERM

SIGNIFICANT DECISIONS OF THE SUPREME COURT, 1976-1977 TERM

Bruce E. Fein

American Enterprise Institute for Public Policy Research
Washington, D.C.

Bruce E. Fein is an attorney with the U.S. Department of Justice.

The views of the author do not necessarily
represent those of the Department of Justice.

Library of Congress Cataloging in Publication Data

Fein, Bruce E
   Significant decisions of the Supreme Court,
1976–1977 term.

   (AEI studies ; 187)
   Includes index.
   1. United States—Constitutional law—Digests.
I. United States. Supreme Court. II. Title.
III. Series: American Enterprise Institute for Public
Policy Research. AEI studies ; 187.
KF4547.8.F422 1978   348′.73′413   78-5056
ISBN 0-8447-3289-3

AEI studies 187

Printed in the United States of America

CONTENTS

1

OVERVIEW

Several critics of the Burger Court have charged it with abdicating its duty to protect minority rights, failing to widen the doors to federal courts to ensure a hospitable reception to federal claims, and declining to police the excesses of majoritarian rule. Some have argued that the 1976–1977 term of the Court supports these charges, pointing to decisions that upheld seniority systems having racially discriminatory effects,[1] embraced a broad application of federal abstention,[2] narrowed the scope of federal habeas corpus review,[3] and rebuffed the constitutional claims of students subject to corporal punishment[4] and of indigents seeking Medicaid reimbursement for elective abortions.[5] Justice Powell's assertion in *Maher* v. *Roe*[6] that the legislature is the appropriate forum in a democracy for resolving the sensitive issue as to whether state funds should subsidize nontherapeutic abortions[7] is cited as illustrative of the callous disregard of the Court for the rights of the disadvantaged. The Court, it is said, is making the constitutional rights of minorities, criminal defendants, consumers, and dissident nonconformists fair game for hostile state judiciaries and legislative bodies. Underlying these attacks is the assumption that

---

[1] International Brotherhood of Teamsters v. United States, 431 U.S. 324 (1977).

[2] Trainor v. Hernandez, 431 U.S. 434 (1977); Juidice v. Vail, 430 U.S. 327 (1977).

[3] Wainwright v. Sykes, 433 U.S. 72 (1977).

[4] Ingraham v. Wright, 430 U.S. 651 (1977).

[5] Maher v. Roe, 432 U.S. 464 (1977); Beal v. Doe, 432 U.S. 438 (1977); Poelher v. Doe, 432 U.S. 519 (1977).

[6] 432 U.S. 464 (1977).

[7] "The decision whether to expend state funds for nontherapeutic abortions is fraught with judgments of policy and value over which opinions are sharply divided. . . . The appropriate forum for [resolving them] in a democracy is the legislature." 432 U.S. 464, 479 (1977).

civil liberties and the rights of the accused will be given short shrift by these institutions and that our freedoms will be dangerously imperiled unless the first line of defense is the federal courts.

These criticisms are overstated and unpersuasive when measured against a careful analysis of the work of the Court and a dispassionate understanding of the constitutional function of legislatures and state courts. They are engendered in part by a failure to understand that the Constitution is vindicated as much in the recognition of its limitations as in its affirmations.[8] Moreover, they denigrate the participatory and educational virtues inherent in the legislative process that nourish a democratic society.

Diverting Federal Litigants to State Courts

In nonconstitutional decisions, the Burger Court has moved over the past seven years on three fronts to reduce the role of the federal courts and increase the prominence of the state judiciaries in the enforcement of federal statutory and constitutional rights. It has enlisted the prudential doctrine of abstention and has narrowly construed federal jurisdictional and habeas corpus statutes in realigning the distribution of the judicial power of the nation.

Abstention. In *Younger* v. *Harris*,[9] the Court held in 1971 that principles of equity jurisprudence and a proper respect for the independence of state courts and state functions require that federal courts abstain from enjoining pending state criminal proceedings on constitutional grounds except in narrowly limited circumstances. An injunction is generally permissible only if the federal plaintiff proves that the state prosecution will cause him great and immediate irreparable harm.[10] Otherwise, his constitutional claims must be presented to the state courts as a defense to the prosecution. These abstention principles ordinarily have equal application when a federal plaintiff seeks declaratory relief against enforcement of state criminal laws on constitutional grounds.[11]

A state prosecution threatens great and immediate irreparable harm if it is brought in bad faith, for purposes of harassment, or pur-

---

[8] See Borella v. Borden, 145 F.2d 63, 65 (2nd Cir. 1944) (Hand, J.), *affirmed* 325 U.S. 679 (1945).

[9] 401 U.S. 37.

[10] If the state fails to provide an impartial forum for hearing a constitutional claim, then the doctrine of abstention has no application. Gibson v. Berryhill, 411 U.S. 564 (1974).

[11] Samuels v. Mackell, 401 U.S. 66 (1971).

suant to a flagrantly unconstitutional statute, or if other extraordinary circumstances are present. This term the Court reaffirmed that the burden of defending against a state prosecution does not of itself justify a federal injunction.[12]

In broadening the application of *Younger* beyond criminal proceedings, the Court has endorsed two aspects of federalism as a foundation: first, it has acknowledged that states have a strong and legitimate interest in effecting their substantive policies without federal interference; second, it has observed that federal interference would reflect negatively on the solemn responsibility, competence, and willingness of state courts to safeguard constitutional rights. Spurred by these concerns, the Court has applied the *Younger* doctrine to state suits seeking abatement of a public nuisance,[13] and, during this term, recovery of welfare monies wrongfully obtained[14] and enforcement of a civil contempt statute.[15] These decisions suggest that federal injunctions against state civil commitment proceedings are also governed by *Younger*.[16] In addition, *Hicks* v. *Miranda*[17] held that *Younger* principles limit the relief available to federal plaintiffs where state criminal proceedings are commenced after the federal complaint is filed, "but before any proceedings of substance on the merits have taken place in the federal court."

A major purpose of the abstention decisions of the Court is to enlarge the role of state courts in the vindication of constitutional rights.

Federal Rules and Jurisdictional Statutes. The Burger Court generally has narrowly construed federal jurisdictional statutes, thereby diverting some suits to the state judiciaries.[18] It has ruled that in class actions raising federal questions or based on diversity jurisdiction, the requirements of 28 U.S. Code 1331 or 1332 are satisfied only if each class member has more than $10,000 in controversy.[19] In *Johnson* v. *Mississippi*,[20] the civil rights removal statute, 28 U.S. Code 1443(1), was virtually demolished as a vehicle for blacks to escape criminal

---

[12] See Trainor v. Hernandez, 431 U.S. 434 (1977).

[13] Huffman v. Pursue, 420 U.S. 592 (1975).

[14] See note 11, above.

[15] Juidice v. Vail, 430 U.S. 327 (1977).

[16] See Lessard v. Schmidt, 414 U.S. 473 (1974).

[17] 422 U.S. 332 (1975).

[18] But see Lynch v. Household Finance Corp., 405 U.S. 538 (1972).

[19] Zahn v. International Paper Co., 414 U.S. 291 (1973).

[20] 421 U.S. 213 (1970).

prosecutions in state courts. The ancillary jurisdiction of federal courts to hear civil rights suits was confined in *Aldinger* v. *Howard*.[21] Additional barriers to federal courts have been erected by the Burger Court in decisions disclaiming inherent judicial authority to award attorneys' fees in suits that vindicate important public policies[22] and burdening class representatives with the costs of notifying prospective class members as a condition to maintaining a class action suit under federal Rule 23(b)(3).[23]

Federal Habeas Corpus Jurisdiction. Under 28 U.S. Code 2241 et seq., federal courts generally have authority to review convictions of state prisoners in habeas corpus proceedings for constitutional defects. In *Stone* v. *Powell*,[24] the Court interpreted the federal habeas statutes to preclude independent review of Fourth Amendment claims if an opportunity for a full and fair hearing of those claims had been afforded in state proceedings. This term, in *Wainwright* v. *Sykes*,[25] the Court repudiated the doctrine of waiver announced fourteen years earlier in *Fay* v. *Noia*.[26] In *Fay*, the Court held that a state prisoner waives his right to raise constitutional claims in federal habeas proceedings only if he "deliberately bypass[es]" legitimate state procedures for presenting those claims to state courts. Deliberate bypass, according to *Fay*, could be established only if the prisoner made a considered choice, after consultation with competent counsel or otherwise, to forgo the privilege of seeking vindication of his federal claims in state courts. In contrast, *Sykes* held that a prisoner's noncompliance with a state rule requiring contemporaneous objection to the admission of constitutionally tainted evidence generally precludes a belated challenge to the evidence in federal habeas proceedings. A federal habeas court, *Sykes* concluded, may entertain such a challenge only if good cause for the noncompliance and actual prejudice engendered by the alleged constitutional violation is established. One year earlier, *Francis* v. *Henderson*[27] held that noncompliance with a state rule requiring that challenges to the composition of a grand jury be made before trial barred a constitutional attack on the grand jury in federal habeas proceedings absent a showing of cause and actual prejudice.

---

[21] 427 U.S. 1 (1976).

[22] Alyeska Pipeline Service Co. v. The Wilderness Society, 421 U.S. 240 (1975).

[23] Eisen v. Carlisle & Jacqueline, 417 U.S. 156 (1974).

[24] 428 U.S. 465 (1976).

[25] 433 U.S. 72 (1977).

[26] 372 U.S. 391 (1963).

[27] 425 U.S. 536 (1976).

Sykes, by disavowing the restrictive waiver doctrine of *Fay*, foreshadows general application of the cause and actual prejudice test to oust federal habeas petitioners advancing constitutional claims that state courts have declined to entertain for noncompliance with a legitimate rule of procedure.

Vindication of Civil Rights, Minority Rights, and Rights of the Accused

It is thought by many that federal courts have a predisposed sympathy and their state counterparts a predisposed hostility to claims of civil rights, minority rights, and rights of the accused. Many recent decisions fail to substantiate this view.

State courts have reached beyond federal constitutional commands in finding state law protections against exclusionary zoning,[28] public school financing based on a local property-tax base,[29] sex discrimination,[30] disclosure of bank records,[31] and the death penalty.[32] Several decisions by state courts resting on state law have conferred rights on criminal suspects that have no counterpart in the U.S. Constitution.[33] At a minimum, this record shows that several state courts are vigorous defenders of civil rights and scrupulous in protecting the rights of criminal suspects. It refutes any blanket charge that the diversion of some federal suits to state courts by the Burger Court is a pretext for belittling constitutional claims. Notably, this diversion is the progeny of prudential concerns and statutory interpretation and lacks any constitutional parentage. Thus, if state courts reveal a pat-

---

[28] Compare Warth v. Seldin, 422 U.S. 490 (1975), with Southern Burlington County NAACP v. Township of Mt. Laurel, 67 N.J. 151, *appeal dismissed and certiorari denied*, 423 U.S. 808 (1975), and appeal of Kit-Mar Builders, Inc., 439 Pa. 466 (1970). Both Michigan and New York require that localities consider regional welfare in adopting zoning ordinances. Green v. Township of Lima, 199 N.W.2d 243 (1972); Berenson v. Town of New Castle, 341 N.E.2d 236 (1975).

[29] Compare San Antonio Independent School District v. Rodriguez, 411 U.S. 1 (1972), with Serano v. Priest, 557 P.2d 929 (Cal. Sup. Ct. 1976), and Horton v. Meskell, 45 U.S.L.W. 2509 (Conn. Sup. Ct. 1977).

[30] Compare Craig v. Boren, 429 U.S. 160 (1977), with Arp v. Workers' Compensation Appeals Board, 45 U.S.L.W. 2557 (Cal. Sup. Ct. 1977).

[31] Compare United States v. Miller, 423 U.S. 435 (1976), and California Bankers Assn. v. Schultz, 416 U.S. 21 (1974), with Burrows v. Superior Court, 13 Cal. 3d 238 (Cal. Sup. Ct. 1974).

[32] Compare Gregg v. Georgia, 428 U.S. 153 (1976), with People v. Anderson, 6 Cal. 3d 628 (Cal. Sup. Ct. 1972).

[33] See William Brennan, "State Constitutions and the Protection of Individual Rights," *Harvard Law Review*, vol. 90 (1977), p. 489.

tern of hostility toward federal rights, no constitutional barrier will prevent the Court or Congress from rechanneling the initial adjudication of federal claims to the federal judiciary.

Moreover, the increased respect accorded state courts by the Burger Court and the greater finality attached to their constitutional adjudications may enhance both the caliber of state judges and their care in protecting federal rights. It is difficult to attract highly qualified judges to state courts when they are treated by the federal judiciary as second-string players who lack the competence to interpret the U.S. Constitution. And some state judges may give hasty and inadequate consideration to constitutional claims in criminal cases if they know a federal habeas court will inevitably adjudicate the claim *de novo*. Disrespect for state courts thus carries the seeds of a self-fulfilling prophecy.[34]

Further, it is important to recognize that the volume of litigation in state courts is on the order of thirty times as great as federal caseloads, and a substantial portion of state litigation undoubtedly requires consideration of federal claims. Because federal review of most of these decisions is impossible, entrustment of constitutional adjudication to state courts is a practical necessity. Thus, decisions by the Burger Court in the areas of abstention, federal jurisdiction, and habeas corpus have arguably enhanced the protection of constitutional rights by assisting, albeit indirectly, in upgrading the state judiciaries.

Deferring to Legislative Bodies

The Burger Court has been criticized for abandoning the role of guardian of minority rights by deferring to the legislative will in areas where controversial and sensitive social policies are implicated. Implicit in this criticism are the assumptions that legislative bodies generally pay little heed to civil liberties and the rights of minorities and that legislative majorities are inclined to act oppressively.

It is true that the Founding Fathers intended the Supreme Court to act as a restraint on legislative bodies.[35] They understood that a majoritarian political process could threaten the rights of minorities,[36]

---

[34] For a contrary balancing of federalism interests, see Burt Neuborne, "The Myth of Parity," *Harvard Law Review*, vol. 90 (1977), p. 1105.

[35] See *The Federalist*, no. 78.

[36] See *The Federalist*, nos. 48, 51; Max Farrand, *The Records of the Federal Convention of 1787*, vol. 2 (New Haven: Yale University Press, 1973), p. 35.

and the Supreme Court was intended in part to prevent tyrannical action by the majority.[37]

There is, however, a perceptible difference between legislative tyranny and reasonable accommodation of competing social interests. The preamble to the Constitution expressly recognizes six potentially conflicting purposes that legislatures may seek to harmonize in struggling with ever-changing but ever-present social problems. In controversial areas where the Burger Court has deferred to the legislative will—financing of abortions by Medicaid,[38] the death penalty for murder,[39] the building of low-income housing,[40] and the financing of public school education,[41] for example—the laws passing constitutional scrutiny were not the offspring of majoritarian overreaching. Rather, they were responsive to conflicting social, political, and economic values that are inherent in a pluralistic community.

The Burger Court has also enlisted the doctrine of standing to channel resolution of disputes away from the federal judiciary and into political forums.[42] Contrary to the assertions of some, legislatures during this period have been receptive to claims of women, minorities, the disadvantaged, and public interest groups. The Voting Rights Act of 1975,[43] the 1972 amendments to the Civil Rights Act of 1964, the Rehabilitation Act of 1973,[44] the Education of the Handicapped Act,[45] the Government in the Sunshine Act,[46] amendments strengthening the antidiscrimination provisions of the 1964 Civil Rights Act,[47] general revenue-sharing legislation,[48] the Crime Control Act[49] and the Equal Credit Opportunity Act[50] are illustrative. In addition, Congress has legislatively reversed Supreme Court decisions resting on nonconstitu-

---

[37] See Raoul Berger, *Congress v. the Supreme Court* (Cambridge: Harvard University Press, 1969), especially pp. 8-12.

[38] See note 5, above.

[39] See note 32, above.

[40] See James v. Valtierra, 402 U.S. 137 (1971).

[41] See note 29, above.

[42] See, for example, Warth v. Seldin, 422 U.S. 490 (1975); United States v. Richardson, 418 U.S. 166 (1974); Schlesinger v. Reservists Committee to Stop the War, 418 U.S. 208 (1974).

[43] P.L. 94-73, 94th Congress, 1st session (1975).

[44] P.L. 93-112, 93rd Congress, 1st session (1973).

[45] P.L. 91-230, 91st Congress, 2d session (1970).

[46] P.L. 94-409, 94th Congress, 2d session (1976).

[47] P.L. 92-261, 92d Congress, 2d session (1972); P.L. 92-318, 92d Congress, 2d session (1972).

[48] P.L., 94-488, 94th Congress, 2d session (1976).

[49] P.L. 94-503, 94th Congress, 2d session (1976).

[50] P.L. 94-239, 94th Congress, 2d session (1976).

tional grounds in order to expand rights of privacy,[51] encourage civil rights litigation,[52] and increase access to government records.[53] State legislatures have recently given shelter to the interests of privacy,[54] newsmen,[55] women,[56] and criminal suspects[57] that is not constitutionally ordained.[58]

The assumption that legislative bodies are uniformly insensitive to the rights of minorities fails to withstand the test of experience. Similarly misguided is the assertion that the Burger Court has given free rein to majoritarian bodies to trample the rights of minorities.

---

[51] In United States v. Bisceglia, 420 U.S. 141 (1975), the Court upheld the authority of the Internal Revenue Service (IRS) to issue a "John Doe" summons calling for the production of books and records that might be relevant to a tax investigation. In the Tax Reform Act of 1976, 26 U.S. Code 7609, Congress limited the issuance of a John Doe summons to circumstances where the IRS satisfies a court that the summons relates to the investigation of an ascertainable group or class of persons, there is reasonable cause to believe that the group has violated an internal revenue law, and the information sought by the summons and the identity of the suspected tax violators are not readily available from other sources.

In Donaldson v. United States, 400 U.S. 517 (1971), the Court held that a taxpayer lacked any statutory right to notice and intervention when the IRS sought records relating to his tax liability through a third-party summons. In the Tax Reform Act of 1976, Congress generally granted taxpayers a right to notice and intervention in judicial proceedings to prevent enforcement of a third-party summons.

[52] In Alyeska Pipeline Service Co. v. The Wilderness Society, 421 U.S. 240 (1975), the Court held that the federal judiciary lacked inherent authority to award attorneys' fees in suits brought to vindicate important public policies. Congress statutorily expanded the authority of federal courts to award attorneys' fees in the Civil Rights Attorneys' Fees Awards Act of 1976, P.L. 94-559, 94th Congress, 2d session (1976). California recently passed legislation authorizing the award of attorneys' fees in an even wider range of public interest litigation. See *The State Bar of California Reports*, October 1977, p. 1.

[53] In EPA v. Mink, 410 U.S. 73 (1973), and FAA v. Robertson, 422 U.S. 255 (1975), the Court broadly construed exemptions one and three of the Freedom of Information Act (FOIA), 5 U.S. Code 552(b)(1), (3), to deny public access to classified records and records whose confidentiality was permitted by other statutes. Congress subsequently amended the FOIA to narrow exemptions one and three. See P.L. 93-502, 93rd Congress, 2d session (1974); P.L. 94-409, 94th Congress, 2d session (1976).

[54] See the California Right to Financial Privacy Act of 1976, "Government," *California Annotated Code*, section 7460 et seq.

[55] Approximately half the states have enacted some type of shield law to protect newsmen from disclosing their sources or from otherwise providing evidence. See *Press Censorship Newsletter*, no. 8 (1975), p. 29.

[56] Since 1971, fourteen states have adopted amendments to state constitutions that expressly prohibit discrimination on account of sex.

[57] Massachusetts enacted a law in 1977 allowing defense attorneys inside grand jury rooms with their clients. *Washington Post*, November 30, 1977.

[58] See United States v. Miller, 425 U.S. 435 (1976); Branzburg v. Hayes, 408 U.S. 665 (1972); Craig v. Boren, 429 U.S. 160 (1977).

Indeed, in the 1976–1977 term, the Court took bold constitutional steps to shield a variety of civil liberties and minority rights from the political process.

It revived the substantive due process doctrine to strike down an East Cleveland ordinance that prohibited a grandmother from residing with two grandsons.[59] Illegitimates were granted preferred status under the equal protection clause in a decision invalidating a statute that denied them intestacy rights upon the deaths of their fathers.[60] The Court generously offered constitutional shelter to aliens in condemning a state statute that disqualified resident aliens who declined to affirm an intent to seek United States citizenship from receiving financial assistance for higher education.[61] Minorities won an important victory in *Casteneda* v. *Partida*,[62] where the Court approved the use of statistical evidence to establish unconstitutional discrimination and refused to relax jurisprudential safeguards against discrimination simply because minority groups occupied important government positions. Blacks benefited from decisions upholding the remedial power of federal judges to order compensatory education programs as part of a desegregation plan[63] and state apportionment plans drawn to create a quota of safe electoral seats for blacks that generally reflects their proportion of the represented population.[64] The constitutional rights of prisoners to medical treatment[65] and access to law libraries[66] were recognized. Males were afforded special protection against sex discrimination,[67] and the constitutionality of benign sex discrimination that prefers women was sustained.[68] The refusal of a Jehovah's Witness to display a state motto on his license plate was accorded First Amendment protection.[69] The Court also endorsed the claims of criminal defendants in decisions further narrowing the circumstances in which the death penalty may be imposed[70] and broadly construing

---

[59] Moore v. City of East Cleveland, 431 U.S. 494 (1977).

[60] Trimble v. Gordon, 430 U.S. 762 (1977).

[61] Nyquist v. Mauclet, 432 U.S. 1 (1977).

[62] 430 U.S. 482 (1977).

[63] Milliken v. Bradley, 433 U.S. 267 (1977).

[64] United Jewish Organization of Williamsburgh, Inc. v. Carey, 430 U.S. 144 (1977).

[65] Estelle v. Gamble, 429 U.S. 97 (1976).

[66] Bounds v. Smith, 430 U.S. 817 (1977).

[67] Craig v. Boren, 429 U.S. 160 (1977).

[68] Califano v. Webster, 430 U.S. 313 (1977).

[69] Wooley v. Maynard, 430 U.S. 705 (1977).

[70] Coker v. Georgia, 433 U.S. 584 (1977); Roberts v. Louisiana, 431 U.S. 633 (1977); Gardner v. Florida, 430 U.S. 349 (1977).

the Sixth Amendment right to counsel.[71] In sum, a careful examination of the 1976–1977 term dispels the notion that the Court has fled from a constitutional duty to prevent majoritarian tyranny.

Those who argue in favor of a predominant federal role in the process of governing would make our liberties rest on shaky ground, reduce participation in and knowledge of government affairs by citizens, and enervate the political processes that are central to a healthy democracy.

An unelected federal judiciary lacks the physical resources necessary to enforce its decrees over the firm opposition of the executive branch and Congress if the latter have general public support.[72] Liberties protected by a judiciary that lacks a modicum of popular approval will be short-lived. In contrast, liberties safeguarded by legislative command have deep roots and will not easily wither. It is thus prudent to make popularly elected legislatures rather than the federal judiciary the primary forum for instilling libertarian values. This goal is undermined when federal courts stretch to remove from the political branches controversial, sensitive, and significant issues of social policy.

Moreover, an activist federal judiciary reduces the involvement of citizens in government. When the Supreme Court constitutionalizes an area of significant social concern, it removes serious discussion of the issues from the political arena. Citizens who know that their legislatures lack power to alter a rule have little incentive to educate themselves or others about the wisdom or implications of it. They may be discouraged from actively participating in political affairs when the federal judiciary leaves an empty plate on the legislative tray. By presumptively deferring to the legislature, the Supreme Court stimulates the concern of citizens with our governing institutions and prompts interested groups to educate the public about pending legislation and other political matters. An informed, involved, and educated electorate is an indispensable ingredient of a healthy and virtuous democracy.

Many critics of the Burger Court fail to perceive the virtues and necessity of substantial reliance on the political process to vindicate the

---

[71] Brewer v. Williams, 430 U.S. 387 (1977).

[72] In Worcestor v. Georgia, 31 U.S. 515 (1832), the Court overturned the convictions of two missionaries who had been prosecuted by Georgia for residing within Indian territory without a state license. With the acquiescence of President Jackson, Georgia officials ignored the mandate of the Court to release the missionaries. They remained in prison for a year until pardoned by the governor of Georgia. See Charles Warren, *The Supreme Court in United States History* (Boston: Little, Brown, and Company, 1922), vol. 2, pp. 217-36; J. Burke, "The Cherokee Cases: A Study in Law, Politics, and Morality," *Stanford Law Review*, vol. 21 (1969), pp. 500, 525, 531.

historic commitment of the nation to liberty and freedom. Their charges are at odds with Justice Holmes's more balanced philosophy of constitutional adjudication:

> Great constitutional provisions must be administered with caution. Some play must be allowed for the joints of the machine, and it must be remembered that legislatures are ultimate guardians of the liberties and welfare of the people in quite as great a degree as the courts.[73]

Guided by this philosophy, the Court during its 1976–1977 term did defer to the legislatures in several controversial areas: abortion,[74] aliens,[75] care of foster children,[76] school discipline,[77] and drugs.[78] As mentioned earlier, however, these decisions were counterbalanced by many others in which the Court frustrated the exercise of majoritarian power. The 1976–1977 term thus reflects a mixture of deference to legislatures and the states and an activist defense of constitutional values that escapes any simple or blanket characterization.

Voting Alignments

The voting patterns of the justices in cases concerning the system of criminal justice, federalism and access to federal courts, and civil rights and civil liberties did not vary appreciably from last term.[79] The one notable development was the movement of Justice Stevens into the liberal bloc of the Court.

In the area of criminal justice, twenty-two significant nonunanimous decisions were selected for examination. Rehnquist offered nary a single vote to the accused or prisoners. Burger voted 19–2 and Blackmun 18–4 in favor of the government. White gave sixteen votes to the government and six to defendants or inmates. Powell and Stewart divided their votes 13–7 and 13–9 respectively to sustain the position of the government. In the liberal bloc, Stevens cast fifteen votes against the government, while Marshall and Brennan rebuffed the government on nineteen occasions each. Compared with last

---

[73] Missouri, Kansas & Texas Ry. Co. v. May, 194 U.S. 267, 270 (1904).

[74] Maher v. Roe, 432 U.S. 464 (1977).

[75] Fiallo v. Bell, 430 U.S. 787 (1977).

[76] Smith v. Organization of Foster Families for Equality and Reform, 431 U.S. 816 (1977).

[77] Ingraham v. Wright, 430 U.S. 651 (1977).

[78] Whalen v. Roe, 429 U.S. 589 (1977).

[79] See Bruce E. Fein, *Significant Decisions of the Supreme Court, 1975-1976 Term* (Washington, D.C.: American Enterprise Institute, 1977), pp. 17-18.

Table 1
ACTION OF INDIVIDUAL JUSTICES

| | Opinions Written[a] | | | | Dissenting Votes[b] | | |
| | | | | | In disposition by | | |
	Opinions of Court	Concur- rences	Dis- sents[c]	Total	Opinion	Memo- randum	Total
Blackmun	14	14	9	37	16	12	28
Brennan	13	13	24	50	51	21	72
Burger	15	11	14	40	23	13	36
Marshall	12	6	21	39	48	19	67
Powell	15	13	10	38	13	7	20
Rehnquist	15	3	15	33	26	18	44
Stevens	13	17	27	57	29	21	50
Stewart	14	7	9	30	24	6	30
White	15	7	11	33	19	7	26
Per curiam	16	—	—	16	—	—	—
Total	142	91	140	373	249	124	373

Note: A complete explanation of the way in which the tables are compiled may be found in "The Supreme Court, 1967 Term," *Harvard Law Review,* vol. 82 (1968), pp. 93, 301-2, and "The Supreme Court, 1969 Term," *Harvard Law Review,* vol. 84 (1970), pp. 30, 254-55.

Table 1, with the exception of the dissenting votes portion, deals only with full-opinion decisions disposing of cases on their merits. Sixteen per curiam decisions were long enough to be considered full opinions. The memorandum tabulations include memorandum orders disposing of cases on the merits by affirming, reversing, vacating, or remanding. They exclude orders disposing of petitions for certiorari, dismissing writs of certiorari as improvidently granted, dismissing appeals for lack of jurisdiction or for lack of a substantial federal question, and disposing of miscellaneous applications. Certified questions are not included.

a A concurrence or dissent is recorded as a written opinion whenever a reason, however brief, is given, except when simply noted by the reporter.

b A justice is considered to have dissented when he voted to dispose of the case in any manner different from that of the majority of the Court.

c Opinions concurring in part and dissenting in part are counted as dissents.

Source: *Harvard Law Review,* vol. 91 (November 1977), p. 295, as corrected.

term, Powell was more disposed and White less disposed to support claims of defendants and prisoners.

Six nonunanimous decisions dealing with issues of federalism or access to federal courts were chosen for scrutiny. The voting patterns were revealing and confirmed the attachment of Stevens to the liberal bloc. Rehnquist endorsed states' rights and limited access to federal courts in all six cases. He was joined by Powell on five occasions and by Burger, Blackmun, and White four times. Stewart split his six votes evenly between national and state authority. Stevens voted to support national interests over those of states in four cases, while Marshall and Brennan voted that way on all occasions but one. Compared with last term, White showed significantly greater hospitality toward state authority, whereas Stevens embraced national powers more frequently.

Twenty nonunanimous decisions involving civil rights and civil liberties were selected for review.[80] Rehnquist and Burger each voted nineteen times against persons seeking constitutional or statutory recognition of asserted civil rights or civil liberties. Stewart declined to embrace such claims fifteen times, while Powell rebuffed plaintiffs in twelve cases. Blackmun divided his twenty votes evenly between sustaining and rejecting civil rights claims. White cast eleven votes and Stevens fourteen in support of civil liberties. Marshall and Brennan each gave nineteen votes to endorse assertions of civil liberties.

These voting patterns and other decisions generally confirm the alignment of the justices last term along the following spectrum, running from judicial conservatism to judicial liberalism as those terms are popularly understood: Rehnquist, Burger, Powell, Blackmun, White, Stewart, Stevens, Marshall, and Brennan. Rehnquist and Burger provide a conservative anchor to the Court. Powell, Blackmun, White, and Stewart add a conservative tilt. Stevens, Marshall, and Brennan generally represent a liberal counterweight to Rehnquist and Burger.

1976–1977 Statistics

The caseload and output of the Supreme Court increased from last term. The total number of cases on dockets fell by 31, from 4,761 to 4,731, while the number disposed of jumped by 112, from 3,806 to 3,918. The number of cases remaining on dockets at the end of the 1976–1977 term dropped by 143, from 955 to 812. The Court heard

---

[80] Issues relating to race, sex, aliens, illegitimates, voting, free speech, and rights of privacy and due process were all embraced by the overarching concept of civil rights and civil liberties for purposes of this review.

Table 2

DISPOSITION OF CASES: 1974, 1975, 1976 OCTOBER TERMS

Number of Cases	1974	1975	1976
Argued during term	175	179	176
Disposed of by full opinions	144	160	154
Disposed of by per curiam opinions	20	16	22
Set for reargument	11	3	0
Granted review during term	172	172	169
Reviewed and decided without oral argument	157	186	207
Total to be available for argument at outset of following term	100	99	88

Source: Office of the Clerk of the Supreme Court of the United States.

176 cases argued, disposed of 154 by signed opinion, and decided 207 cases without oral argument. The corresponding figures for the 1975–1976 term were 179 cases argued, 160 disposed of by signed opinion, and 186 cases decided without oral argument.

2
SUMMARIES OF
SIGNIFICANT DECISIONS

Criminal Law: Powers of the Police and Prosecutors

Crime continues to plague the nation, with varying intensity in particular states and municipalities.[1] Against this background, the decisions of the Court during the 1976–1977 term declined invitations to impose additional constitutional limitations on investigative and prosecutorial powers. Interpreting the Constitution to embody a restrictive code of conduct for law enforcement personnel should be disfavored for two reasons. First, preserving domestic tranquility and maintaining the blessings of liberty are constitutionally endorsed[2] as legitimate responsibilities of government. Constitutional provisions, such as the Fourth Amendment, that are designed to shield the citizenry from overzealous investigators or prosecutors are generally drafted in broad language, with room to accommodate the legitimate societal interest in deterring crime, as well as the individual interests in privacy and a fair trial. Rules throughout the field of criminal law generally strike a balance among these competing values. A constitutional rule imposed by the Supreme Court, however, has serious drawbacks because it freezes the balance at a particular point in time. Constitutional rules ordinarily do not rise or fall with the severity of the crime problem or the frequency of police or prosecutorial abuses. Legislative rules, in contrast, can be responsive to altered conditions and can make corresponding adjustments in the criminal law balance.

---

[1] In 1975, for example, the rate of violent crimes per 100,000 persons ranged from 53.1 in North Dakota to 856 in New York. See Federal Bureau of Investigation, *Crime in the United States*, 1975 Uniform Crime Reports, pp. 49-55.

[2] The preamble to the Constitution embraces as two of its majestic purposes insuring "domestic Tranquility" and securing "the Blessings of Liberty."

Second, a constitutional rule is by definition a nationwide rule. It is not generally responsive to the countless variations in crime and police problems in different states and localities or to law enforcement problems unique to the federal government. The medicine it offers, therefore, will inevitably be both too strong and too weak, depending on the community. Legislative treatment of crime problems, in contrast, can adapt to distinctive law enforcement problems among federal, state, and local jurisdictions.

Of course, these considerations do not justify abdication of the responsibility of the Court to protect individual rights and to require adherence to fundamental procedural safeguards. But they are sufficiently weighty to justify a presumptive reluctance to impose constitutional rules over detailed aspects of the nation's criminal justice procedures.

This view was generally endorsed by the Court in eight significant decisions this term pertaining to investigative and prosecutorial powers. In six decisions, the interest of the government in detecting crimes and convicting criminals was vindicated. The unifying constitutional theme of these decisions was best expressed by Justice White in *Patterson* v. *New York*, 432 U.S. 197 (1977): "Traditionally, due process has required that only the most basic procedural safeguards be observed; more subtle balancing of society's interests against those of the accused have been left to the legislative branch." But in two other decisions the Court rebuffed government attempts to constrict fundamental Fourth Amendment protections.

None of the six decisions favorable to the government broke new ground. In *Patterson* v. *New York*, the Court sustained a statute requiring a defendant charged with second-degree murder to carry the burden of proving the affirmative defense of acting under the influence of extreme emotional disturbance. *Patterson* repudiated any intimation in *Mullaney* v. *Wilbur*, 421 U.S. 684 (1975),[3] that due process might require the government to prove beyond a reasonable doubt any fact whose existence triggers a significant increase or decrease in criminal culpability or punishment.

In *Oregon* v. *Mathiason*, 429 U.S. 492 (1977), the Court placed another limiting interpretation on *Miranda* v. *Arizona*, 384 U.S. 436 (1966).[4] It declined to require *Miranda* warnings before interrogation

---

[3] There a due process defect was found in a statute that required an accused charged with felonious homicide to prove the existence of sudden provocation to justify punishing the crime as manslaughter.

[4] See, for example, United States v. Mandujano, 425 U.S. 564 (1976); Michigan v. Mosley, 423 U.S. 96 (1975); Oregon v. Haas, 420 U.S. 714 (1975); Harris v. New York, 401 U.S. 222 (1971).

of suspects who voluntarily submit to questioning in a police station. Eschewing inflexible exclusionary rules, *Manson v. Brathwaite*, 432 U.S. 98 (1977), upheld the admissibility of photo identification evidence that was reliable, even though it was obtained through the use of unnecessarily suggestive procedures.

The Court gave constitutional endorsement to the longstanding tradition of border searches in *United States v. Ramsey*, 431 U.S. 606 (1977). It rejected a Fourth Amendment attack on a federal statute authorizing customs officials to search incoming international mail if there is "reasonable cause" to suspect contraband. Lurking in the background of the *Ramsey* decision was the explosive growth in international smuggling of drugs.

Fearful of shackling the investigative process, *United States v. Lovasco*, 431 U.S. 783 (1977), declined to find any constitutional defect in deferring an indictment in order to trace all leads and to uncover additional criminal participants. Any prejudice to the defendant caused by such delays, the Court reasoned, was not of constitutional dimension.

The Court expressed irritation over the careless disregard by the government of statutory controls on the use of wiretaps in *United States v. Donovan*, 429 U.S. 413 (1977). There the government improperly omitted the names of three of a large number of persons suspected of illegal gambling in obtaining a wiretap warrant. Upon termination of the wiretaps, the government unlawfully failed to inform the judge of two persons whose conversations had been intercepted. *Donovan* held that these statutory violations were insufficiently important to trigger suppression of evidence derived from the wiretaps. *Donovan* hinted, however, that purposeful violations, or even a persistence of negligent infractions, would force the Court to embrace a suppression remedy.[5]

The Court stood firm against overreaching by government in *United States v. Chadwick*, 433 U.S. 1 (1977), and *G.M. Leasing Corp. v. United States*, 429 U.S. 338 (1977). In the former, the Court sharply repudiated the government's quest to exclude movable personal property seized in public places from fundamental Fourth Amendment protections. In the latter, a search of corporate books and property by the Internal Revenue Service was condemned under

---

[5] Wiretaps and electronic surveillance have spawned a host of novel judicial and prosecutorial problems. The late Chief Justice Earl Warren recounted a bizarre episode in which the attorney general by proxy made a blatantly improper *ex parte* contact with the Court to inform it of the existence of warrantless electronic surveillance of numerous embassies. See *The Memoirs of Chief Justice Earl Warren* (New York: Doubleday & Company, 1977), pp. 337-42.

the Fourth Amendment. Corporations and corporate premises do not forfeit their Fourth Amendment shield, the Court reasoned, simply because delinquent taxes are owed.

Patterson v. *New York*, 432 U.S. 197 (1977)

Facts: Under New York law, second-degree murder consists of two elements: "intent to cause the death of another person" and "caus[ing] the death of such person or of a third person." New York provides an affirmative defense to a charge of murder if the accused proves by a preponderance of the evidence that he "acted under the influence of extreme emotional disturbance for which there was a reasonable explanation or excuse." The separate crime of manslaughter under New York law reaches homicides committed under the influence of extreme emotional disturbance. Convicted of second-degree murder, Patterson appealed, claiming that due process prohibited the state from placing the burden of proving an affirmative defense on the accused. The New York Court of Appeals rejected the claim.

Question: Does constitutional due process prohibit New York from placing the burden of proving an affirmative defense to a charge of second-degree murder on the accused?

Decision: No. Opinion by Justice White. Vote: 6–3, Brennan, Marshall, and Powell dissenting.

Reasons: State laws regulating the administration of criminal justice pass scrutiny under the due process clause unless they offend fundamental principles of justice deeply rooted in the traditions and conscience of the people. The burden of proving affirmative defenses resting on circumstances of justification, excuse, or alleviation was routinely placed on the accused when the Fifth Amendment was adopted and the Fourteenth Amendment was ratified. In *Leland* v. *Oregon*, 343 U.S. 790 (1952), and *Rivera* v. *Delaware*, 429 U.S. 877 (1976), the Court sustained the constitutionality of state laws requiring the defendant to prove the defense of insanity.

This case is indistinguishable from *Leland* and *Rivera*. The state was required to prove beyond a reasonable doubt the two elements of the crime of second-degree murder. At that point, due process permitted the state to decline to recognize an affirmative defense that would mitigate the degree of culpability and punishment unless established by the accused. As in *Leland* and *Rivera*, proof of the affirmative defense would not negate any of the facts required to prove murder.

Due process requires a state to prove beyond a reasonable doubt all factual elements of a crime. Thereafter, a state may recognize mitigating factors affecting culpability and punishment free from the restraints of the reasonable doubt rule. It may require the accused to prove a mitigating circumstance if the proof of its nonexistence by the state would be "too cumbersome, too expensive, and too inaccurate."

> We thus decline to adopt as a constitutional imperative, operative country-wide, that a State must disprove beyond reasonable doubt every fact constituting any and all affirmative defenses related to the culpability of the accused. Traditionally, due process has required that only the most basic procedural safeguards be observed; more subtle balancing of society's interests against those of the accused have been left to the legislative branch.

The Court asserted that its decision was consistent with *Mullaney* v. *Wilbur*, 421 U.S. 684 (1975), in which a Maine homicide statute was held unconstitutional because it defined murder as the intentional killing of another in the absence of provocation, but failed to require the state to prove the absence of provocation beyond a reasonable doubt. The controlling fact in *Mullaney* was the choice by the state of making the absence of provocation part of the definition of the crime of murder.

Oregon v. *Mathiason*, 429 U.S. 492 (1977)

Facts: A burglary suspect voluntarily met with police in a state patrol office and submitted to interrogation after being advised that he was not under arrest. The suspect confessed after the police stated falsely that his fingerprints were found at the scene of the crime. The confession was used to obtain a burglary conviction in spite of the claim that its suppression was required because the police failed to give the warnings mandated by *Miranda* v. *Arizona*, 384 U.S. 436 (1966). The Oregon Supreme Court overturned the conviction, reasoning that since interrogation of the suspect occurred in a "coercive environment," *Miranda* warnings were constitutionally required.

Question: Was the questioned confession obtained in violation of *Miranda* v. *Arizona*?

Decision: No. Per curiam opinion. Vote: 6–3, Brennan, Marshall, and Stevens dissenting.

Reasons: Miranda warnings are required only when police interrogation occurs after a person "has been taken into custody or otherwise deprived of his freedom in any significant way." In this case, the suspect was neither under arrest nor otherwise under physical restraint by the police when the questioned interrogation commenced. *Miranda* does not apply simply because interrogation occurs in a coercive environment:

> Any interview of one suspected of a crime by a police officer will have coercive aspects to it, simply by virtue of the fact that the police officer is part of a law enforcement system which may ultimately cause the suspect to be charged with a crime. But police officers are not required to administer Miranda warnings to everyone whom they question.

Manson v. *Brathwaite,* 432 U.S. 98 (1977)

Facts: Standing in a lighted hallway, a trained black undercover police officer purchased heroin from the accused through an open doorway. A short time later, he returned to police headquarters and described the accused to another officer. On the basis of that description, the undercover officer was given a photograph of the accused, whom he identified two days later as the seller of the heroin. This pretrial photo identification was used as evidence to convict the accused of narcotics charges.

The prosecution failed to explain why neither a photographic array of several persons nor a line-up was used to obtain a more reliable identification. A federal court of appeals overturned the conviction in habeas corpus proceedings, concluding that the pretrial photo identification was unnecessarily suggestive and thus its use as evidence violated due process.

Question: Does the use of unnecessarily suggestive identification evidence in a criminal prosecution by itself violate due process?

Decision: No. Opinion by Justice Blackmun. Vote: 7–2, Brennan and Marshall dissenting.

Reasons: In *Stovall* v. *Denno,* 388 U.S. 293 (1967), the Court concluded that due process proscribed the use of identification evidence that derived from unnecessarily suggestive procedures, at least where the procedures created a likelihood of mistaken identification. *Neil v. Biggers*, 409 U.S. 188 (1972), held that due process permitted the use of all identification evidence that was reliable considering the totality of circumstances, at least with regard to pre-*Stovall* evidence. A balancing of interests requires application of the *Biggers* rule to post-*Stovall* evidence as well. To exclude reliable identification evidence simply because unnecessarily suggestive procedures were used would allow some guilty persons to go free; at the same time, its deterrent effect on improper police practices would be marginal. "Inflexible rules of exclusion that may frustrate rather than promote justice have not been viewed recently by this Court with unlimited enthusiasm."

In determining the reliability of identification evidence, the following factors should be considered:

> the opportunity of the witness to view the criminal at the time of the crime, the witness' degree of attention, the accuracy of his prior description of the criminal, the level of certainty demonstrated at the confrontation, and the time between the crime and the confrontation. Against these factors is to be weighed the corrupting effect of the suggestive identification itself.

Under the circumstances of this case, photo identification by the undercover officer was sufficiently reliable to satisfy due process. Although single-photograph displays are suspect and less reliable than multiple displays of photographs or line ups, their use does not inexorably contravene due process standards of fundamental fairness.

United States v. *Ramsey*, 431 U.S. 606 (1977)

Facts: Under 19 U.S. Code 482, customs officials are authorized to search incoming international mail if there is "reasonable cause to suspect" that it contains material imported unlawfully. A customs officer invoked the statute to justify his search of eight bulky letters sent from Thailand, a known source of narcotics. Heroin was discovered in the envelopes, which were subsequently resealed and delivered. Federal agents used this knowledge to bring about the arrest and indictment of two persons for violation of federal law. The defendants were found guilty after the district court denied their motion to suppress the heroin on the ground that it was discovered in violation of the Fourth Amendment. The court of appeals reversed, holding that the Fourth Amendment requires a showing of probable cause and a search warrant before a government official may open international letter mail.

Question: Does the Fourth Amendment require customs officers to obtain a search warrant based on probable cause before opening international letter mail at the U.S. border?

Decision: No. Opinion by Justice Rehnquist. Vote: 6–3, Stevens, Brennan, and Marshall dissenting.

Reasons: The Fourth Amendment prohibits only unreasonable searches. Ordinarily, searches are unreasonable unless accompanied by a warrant issued upon probable cause by a neutral magistrate. It has been well established since the birth of the United States, however, that border searches of persons and property entering the country "are reasonable simply by virtue of the fact that they occur at the border." No different rule is justified for incoming letter mail. The border-search exception to the general Fourth Amendment requirements of probable cause and a warrant "is grounded in the recognized right of the sovereign to control, subject to substantive limitations imposed by the Constitution, who and what may enter the country." To afford enhanced Fourth Amendment border protection to incoming letter mail would be inconsistent with this rationale.

United States v. *Lovasco,* 431 U.S. 783 (1977)

Facts: A district court dismissed a federal firearms indictment obtained eighteen months after the alleged commission of the offenses. It found that the deaths of two material witnesses during the preindictment delay prejudiced the defense and that the government had sufficient evidence to indict within one month of the alleged offenses. Thus, the district court reasoned, the prosecution violated due process. The court of appeals affirmed.

Question: Does due process require dismissal of an indictment if preindictment delay prejudices the defendant and is justified solely by the desire of the government to continue an investigation?

Decision: No. Opinion by Justice Marshall. Vote: 8–1, Stewart dissenting.

Reasons: In *United States* v. *Marion,* 404 U.S. 307 (1971), the Court concluded that due process might prohibit intentional manipulation by the government of preaccusation delay to prejudice the defendant. *Marion* made clear that both prejudice and the reasons for delay must be considered in assessing a due process claim. Here the challenged delay resulted from the government's hope that continued investigation might reveal additional participants in the firearms violations. Due process does not require a prosecutor to indict as soon as he believes that probable cause or proof beyond a reasonable doubt exists. To impose such a duty would encourage unwarranted indictments and duplicative trials stemming from a single criminal scheme and would obstruct the successful detection and prosecution of large conspiracies. Investigative delay may work to benefit either a suspect or the government. A prosecutor adheres to elementary standards of fair play by refusing

> to seek indictments until he is completely satisfied that he should prosecute and will be able promptly to establish guilt beyond a reasonable doubt. . . . We therefore hold that to prosecute a defendant following investigative delay does not deprive him of due process, even if his defense might have been somewhat prejudiced by the lapse of time.

United States v. Donovan, 429 U.S. 413 (1977)

Facts: Title III of the Omnibus Crime Control and Safe Streets Act of 1968, 18 U.S. Code 2510–2520, establishes an elaborate statutory scheme for the issuance of judicial warrants authorizing wiretaps. Under 18 U.S. Code 2518(1)(b)(iv), the government must include in its wiretap applications "the identity of the person, if known, committing the offense [under investigation], and whose conversations are to be intercepted." Under 18 U.S. Code 2518(8)(d), a judge is generally required, after a specified period, to give notice to persons named in wiretap applications and to indicate whether their communications were intercepted. In addition, the provision authorizes the judge to give notice to other persons whose conversations were intercepted if he concludes that such action is in the interest of justice.

The government obtained a wiretap warrant to investigate certain illegal gambling activities, but inadvertently failed in its wiretap application to name three persons involved. In addition, after the wiretaps had been terminated, the government failed to inform the judge of two persons whose conversations had been intercepted but who were not named in the wiretap application. After their indictment for federal gambling violations, these five persons moved to suppress evidence derived from the wiretaps under 18 U.S. Code 2518(10)(a). They claimed, respectively, that the wiretaps were obtained in violation of section 2518(1)(b)(iv) because of the failure to name in the application all persons known and involved and were conducted in violation of section 2518(8)(d) because of the failure to inform the judge of all persons whose conversations had been intercepted. The district court granted both motions and the court of appeals affirmed.

Questions: (1) Did the government obtain and conduct the questioned wiretaps in violation of sections 2518(1)(b)(iv) and 2518 (8) (d)? (2) If so, does section 2518(10)(a) require suppression of the evidence derived from the wiretaps?

Decision: Yes to the first question and no to the second. Opinion by Justice Powell. Vote: 6–3, Marshall, Brennan, and Stevens dissenting.

Reasons: With regard to the wiretap application issue, section 2518(1)(b)(iv) plainly requires the government to identify all persons it has probable cause to believe are engaged in the criminal activity under investigation and whose conversations will be intercepted. The government argues that this identification requirement extends only to persons who will actually use the telephone to be wiretapped. That interpretation must be rejected as unsupportable by legislative history and inconsistent with the carefully constructed wiretap scheme in Title III.

Similarly, legislative history and statutory purpose compel the conclusion that section 2518(8)(d) requires the government to inform the judge of all persons whose conversations were intercepted. This is necessary to enable the judge to determine whether notice should be provided in the interest of justice. To discharge this obligation, a judge, at a minimum, requires knowledge of persons or categories of persons whose conversations were overheard. The government violated section 2518(8)(d) in failing to inform the judge of two persons whose conversations were intercepted by the judicially authorized wiretaps.

Violations of Title III, however, do not automatically trigger suppression of evidence derived from the wiretaps. Section 2518(10)(a), as relevant to this case, requires suppression only of communications that were "unlawfully intercepted." In *United States* v. *Chavez*, 416 U.S. 562 (1974), the Court concluded that a violation of a Title III provision did not make an interception unlawful unless the provision plays a "substantive role" in the regulatory system governing court-authorized wiretaps.

Here the failure of the government to identify three of a large number of persons in its wiretap application played no "substantive role" with regard to the judicial decision to issue a wiretap warrant.

The application contained a full and complete statement of the criminal activity under investigation, the types of conversations to be intercepted, and a large number of the wiretap targets. "In no meaningful sense can it be said that the presence of . . . information as to additional targets would have precluded judicial authorization of the intercept." Likewise, the postintercept notice requirement was not intended to restrain issuance of wiretap warrants but to "assure the community that the wiretap technique is reasonably employed." Its violation does not render an intercept unlawful, thereby triggering suppression under section 2518(10)(a).

Indicating that suppression might be required for a purposeful violation, as opposed to an inadvertent violation, of Title III, the Court reiterated the warning given in *United States* v. *Chavez* that "strict adherence by the Government to the provisions of Title III would . . . be more in keeping with the responsibilities Congress has imposed upon it when authority to engage in wiretapping or electronic surveillance is sought."

United States v. *Chadwick*, 433 U.S. 1 (1977)

Facts: Federal narcotics agents arrested Chadwick and others for unlawful possession of marijuana with intent to distribute. The arrests were made near a waiting automobile that contained a 200-pound footlocker in its open trunk. With probable cause to believe the footlocker contained marijuana, the agents took it to a federal building, opened it without obtaining a warrant, and discovered large amounts of marijuana. Before Chadwick's trial, a federal district court suppressed use of the marijuana on the ground that the warrantless search of the footlocker violated the Fourth Amendment. The court of appeals affirmed. It rejected the government's contention that warrantless searches of movable personal property lawfully seized in a public place pass Fourth Amendment scrutiny if there is probable cause to believe the property contains evidence of crime.

Question: Did the warrantless search of the footlocker violate the Fourth Amendment?

Decision: Yes. Opinion by Chief Justice Burger. Vote: 7–2, Blackmun and Rehnquist dissenting.

Reasons: The Fourth Amendment prohibits "unreasonable" searches and seizures. Subject to narrow exceptions, it requires officials to obtain a warrant based on probable cause and issued by a neutral magistrate before searching for evidence of crime. Neither the language nor the fundamental privacy values underlying the Fourth Amendment justify a wholesale exclusion of movable personal property from the warrant requirement.

Here no recognized exception excused the failure to obtain a warrant. The agents exercised exclusive control over the footlocker after its seizure and had no reason to believe that it contained inherently dangerous items or evidence that would lose value unless immediately secured. Thus the exigent circumstances exception was inapplicable.

Chimel v. *California*, 395 U.S. 752 (1969), permits warrantless searches of areas within the immediate control of an arrestee to prevent his destruction of evidence or seizure of a weapon. But *Chimel* could not validate the contested search because it occurred without danger that Chadwick or his associates might seize a weapon or destroy evidence in the footlocker.

Finally, warrantless searches of automobiles are generally permitted because of their inherent mobility and the lesser expectations of privacy surrounding their use. Automobiles are predominantly used for transportation, not as a repository of personal effects, and both their occupants and contents are frequently exposed to the public. In contrast to the inherent mobility of automobiles, however, the footlocker was safely immobilized when the search occurred. Footlockers are intended to carry personal effects, moreover, and their use carries a correspondingly higher expectation of privacy than does the use of motor vehicles. The reasons justifying the exception to the requirement that a warrant be obtained for automobile searches cannot excuse the warrantless search of the footlocker. Accordingly, it was constitutionally defective under the Fourth Amendment.

G.M. Leasing Corp. v. *United States*, 429 U.S. 338 (1977)

Facts: Under 26 U.S. Code 6861(a) the Internal Revenue Service (IRS) made jeopardy assessments against a taxpayer for alleged deficiencies in income tax payments.[6] After failing to obtain payment, the IRS sought to collect the unpaid taxes by levy upon the taxpayer's property as authorized by 26 U.S. Code 6331(a). Levy includes the power of distraint and seizure by any means of all types of property—real and personal, tangible and intangible. Invoking

---

[6] That section authorizes immediate tax assessments if the service believes that the collection of a deficiency would be jeopardized by delay.

this power, the IRS seized the taxpayer's automobiles, searched his business premises, and seized various books and records to obtain information relating to the location of other assets. Both the automobiles and the premises were nominally held in the name of a sham corporation. Thereafter, the corporation brought suit seeking damages, claiming that the seizures of the vehicles and its books and records without a warrant violated the Fourth Amendment prohibition against unreasonable searches and seizures. That claim was rejected by a federal court of appeals.

Questions: Did the Fourth Amendment prohibit the warrantless seizures of the automobiles? Of the books and records?

Decision: No to the first question and yes to the second. Opinion by Justice Blackmun for a unanimous Court.

Reasons: It is conceded that there was probable cause to believe that the automobiles were properly subject to seizure in satisfaction of the tax assessments. Because the seizures took place in open places and involved no invasion of privacy, a judicial warrant was not required under the doctrine of *Murray's Lessee* v. *Hoboken Land & Improv. Co.,* 18 How. 272 (1856). There the Court held that a warrantless transfer of a debtor's land in satisfaction of a claim of the United States was constitutionally permissible.

In contrast to the automobile seizures, however, the seizures of the corporation's books and records involved a significant intrusion into the privacy of its business offices. Both corporations and business premises are protected by the Fourth Amendment. Absent exigent circumstances, the amendment generally requires a judicial warrant that is based on probable cause before premises can be searched. The IRS failed to prove that its warrantless search of the corporation's premises was justified by any constitutionally recognized exigency.

Criminal Law: Rights of the Accused

Many have characterized the Burger Court as insensitive to the constitutional rights of the accused. Some have charged it with watering down constitutional protections and ignoring the dangers of police or prosecutorial abuses. These claims, however, find little support in the moderate decisions of this term in five major areas that implicate constitutional protections of the accused: the death penalty, the guarantee against double jeopardy, the privilege against compulsory self-incrimination, the right to counsel, and obscenity.

Death Penalty. The Court began the process of filling in the many gaps left open by the controversial death penalty cases of last term [7] in confronting three new issues.[8] Its most controversial and intellectually deficient decision, *Coker* v. *Georgia*, 433 U.S. 584 (1977), enlisted the Eighth Amendment prohibition of cruel and unusual punishment to invalidate a death sentence imposed for rape, after a jury had carefully considered all aggravating and mitigating circumstances. The plurality opinion of Justice White reflected an inability or unwillingness to deal dispassionately with the question of the death penalty.

Coker could certainly be called a recidivist. He had committed two earlier rapes, murder, kidnapping, and aggravated assault and had escaped from a prison where he was serving three life sentences before perpetrating the rape for which he was condemned to die.[9] There seem at least two reasons for imposing capital punishment on such a violent recidivist.[10] First, the lesser punishment of life imprisonment for one already serving three life sentences is tantamount to no punishment at all. Its threat provides no deterrent to prison escapes and additional crimes. Second, the threat of the death penalty arguably would deter some potential rapists, in part by instructing the citizenry of the community's stern disapproval of the crime.[11]

Justice White, however, did not make even a perfunctory acknowledgment of these legitimate interests. Instead, he moved directly to the conclusion that the death penalty for rape is "grossly disproportionate and excessive punishment" and thus forbidden by the Eighth Amendment. The march of history, he said, was against the death penalty for rape. Georgia was the sole jurisdiction authorizing death for the rape of an adult women, and only two other states threatened capital punishment for the rape of a child. Justice White failed to perceive, however, that history does not march in a single

---

[7] See Gregg v. Georgia, 428 U.S. 153 (1976), Proffitt v. Florida, 428 U.S. 242 (1976), and Jurek v. Texas, 428 U.S. 262 (1976) (all upholding the death penalty for murder when administered pursuant to procedural safeguards), and Woodson v. North Carolina, 428 U.S. 280 (1976) and Roberts v. Louisiana, 428 U.S. 325 (1976) (striking down mandatory death penalty statutes).

[8] In Roberts v. Louisiana, 431 U.S. 633 (1977), the Court invalidated a mandatory death penalty statute triggered by the murder of a policeman. This result was required by Woodson v. North Carolina.

[9] 433 U.S. 605 (Burger, C. J., dissenting).

[10] The threat of a death penalty may also encourage conspirators to cooperate with the prosecution in return for a noncapital charge. This apparently occurred in the investigation of the murder of United Mine Workers dissident Jock Yablonski.

[11] A majority of the public believes the threat of the death penalty deters crime. See note 13, below.

direction. During the past decade, public opinion, responding to a mushrooming crime rate,[12] has dramatically altered its position on the death penalty from opposition to strong support.[13] Giving due consideration to the sluggishness of the legislative process, it would seem speculative to infer a permanent societal opposition to the death penalty for rape simply because at any particular time only a few states have such laws.

Second, Justice White noted that juries in Georgia failed to impose capital punishment for rape in at least nine out of ten cases. The inference he drew was that juries generally reject the acceptability of death as a penalty for rape. An equally plausible inference, however, is that juries, acting under constitutionally mandated safeguards,[14] are scrupulous in separating the heinous, recidivist offender from those posing a lesser threat to society.

Finally, the plurality observed that the murderer kills while the rapist does not. This, however, is an observation, not a reason. It says little or nothing about the acceptability of capital punishment for the crime of rape when aggravating circumstances abound.

Although the holding of Coker is difficult to accept on the merits of the decision, some have misinterpreted its implications in asserting that it precludes the death penalty for any crime but murder. The plurality, however, did not rule out the death penalty for such crimes as treason, espionage, skyjacking, or certain terrorist activities.[15]

Last term the Court erected several constitutional safeguards to protect the rights of a convicted murderer during the sentencing stage where death is a possibility.[16] This term in Gardner v. Florida, 430 U.S. 349 (1977), the Court provided an additional protection in holding that due process prohibits reliance on an undisclosed presentence report to impose capital punishment. The Court reasoned

---

[12] The crime rate more than doubled between 1965 and 1975 for seven categories of serious offenses reported to the Federal Bureau of Investigation. See Federal Bureau of Investigation, Crime in the United States, 1976 Uniform Crime Reports, p. 49.

[13] A CBS-New York Times poll conducted in June 1977 showed public approval of the death penalty by a 73 percent to 21 percent margin (transcript of CBS Evening News, August 2, 1977). In 1966, a Gallup poll found a plurality of 42 percent opposed to the death penalty.

[14] See Gregg v. Georgia, 428 U.S. 153 (1976).

[15] This is because the plurality rested its decision primarily on a perceived societal rejection of the death penalty for rape. There is no comparable evidence that society has generally rejected death as an acceptable penalty for these crimes, at least when accompanied by aggravating circumstances.

[16] See Gregg v. Georgia, Proffitt v. Florida, and Jurek v. Texas, note 7, above.

that the uniqueness of the death sentence justified departing from the general principle of *Williams* v. *New York*,[17] namely that due process permits confidential information contained in presentence reports to be used by a judge in exercising his sentencing authority.

In the third death penalty decision, *Dobbert* v. *Florida*, 432 U.S. 282 (1977), the Court confronted an ex post facto challenge to the retroactive application of death penalty procedures. So long as the new death penalty procedures generally offer greater protections than existed under prior law, the Court reasoned, they satisfy ex post facto scrutiny, even though a procedural device in the old law would have saved a particular convict from the death sentence.

Further inconsistency on death penalty issues can be expected from the Court in future terms; it is an area that stirs strong emotions. But it would be wrong for the Court to assume that the political branches of government or the public cannot grapple rationally with the issue. The execution of Gary Gilmore has not unleashed the unreasoning forces or widespread executions that some predicted. The lesson of recent history is that capital punishment for vicious crimes by repeat offenders becomes publicly acceptable when an intolerable number of law-abiding citizens are victimized and efforts at rehabilitation appear to have proved fruitless. The interpretation of the Eighth Amendment should be informed by the recognition that the "Constitution is not a suicide pact." [18]

Double Jeopardy. The Court generously construed the double jeopardy clause in two cases in which the accused prevailed. In *Brown* v. *Ohio*, 432 U.S. 161 (1977), the Court held that the clause barred separate prosecutions for both a greater and lesser included offense, whatever the sequence in which the defendant is prosecuted. The double jeopardy clause was also invoked, in *United States* v. *Martin Linen Supply Co.*, 430 U.S. 564 (1977), to bar the government's appeal of a judgment of acquittal entered by a trial judge for insufficient evidence, after a deadlocked jury was discharged.

In *Lee* v. *United States*, 432 U.S. 23 (1977), however, the Court found no constitutional objection to a retrial after the accused obtained a dismissal because of defective information. And by a narrow margin of 5–4, the Court rejected, in *Jeffers* v. *United States*, 432 U.S. 137 (1977), a double jeopardy claim based on the rule of *Brown* v. *Ohio*, by denying its protection to defendants who successfully object to the joint trial of the greater and lesser offenses.

---

[17] 337 U.S. 241 (1949).

[18] See *Terminiello* v. *Chicago*, 337 U.S. 1, 57 (1949) (Jackson, J., dissenting).

Self-Incrimination. Watergate and its aftermath have ushered in a period of heightened public concern with the integrity of public officials and the political process. In *Lefkowitz* v. *Cunningham*, 431 U.S. 801 (1977), the Court, nevertheless, overturned a state statute that ousted officials of political parties from office and barred them from holding office for five years if they invoked the Fifth Amendment privilege against self-incrimination. It held that a state was constitutionally barred from advancing its compelling interest in maintaining public confidence in the political process by coercing politicians to waive the Fifth Amendment privilege. A constitutional path to the state's goal remained open, the Court observed, since the testimony of a party official could be obtained if he was granted use immunity from criminal prosecution.

In *United States* v. *Washington*, 431 U.S. 181 (1977), the Court declined to extend Fifth Amendment protection to require the warning of a grand jury witness that he was a target of the investigation.

Right to Counsel. After arrest, an accused has a right to counsel during any police interrogation. This term, in *Brewer* v. *Williams*, 430 U.S. 387 (1977), a bitterly divided Court overturned a murder conviction based on a confession obtained in the absence of the arrestee's counsel. A so-called Christian burial speech made by a police officer elicited a confession in the absence of counsel by playing on the sympathies of the arrestee. The dissenters argued that the speech was not tantamount to interrogation.[19]

The use of undercover agents was attacked in *Weatherford* v. *Bursey*, 429 U.S. 545 (1977), in which an agent was arrested and attended strategy meetings with a codefendant and the codefendant's counsel to preserve his cover for future law enforcement use. Since the agent neither transmitted to the prosecution nor testified to any information derived from the meetings, the Court rejected the contention that his participation violated the Sixth Amendment right of the codefendant to counsel.

Obscenity. The treatment of obscenity issues by the Court has followed a checkered course. In 1973, it expanded the constitutional scope of obscenity while requiring greater specificity in the prohibition of obscene materials.[20] In *Marks* v. *United States*, 430 U.S.

---

[19] The accused was subsequently convicted of murder again on retrial. District Court of the State of Iowa in and for Polk County (Cr. 58805 1977) (Judge Denato).

[20] Miller v. California, 413 U.S. 15 (1973).

31

188 (1977), the Court held that due process forbade retroactive criminal application of an expanded definition of obscenity. It marked one of the few occasions on which all nine justices agreed in the result of an obscenity decision. In *Smith* v. *United States*, 431 U.S. 291 (1977), however, the Court could muster only five votes to reaffirm an earlier holding that local community standards are to be used in determining whether material is obscene under federal obscenity laws.

Coker v. *Georgia*, 433 U.S. 584 (1977)

Facts: Coker escaped from a Georgia prison in which he was serving three life sentences, two twenty-year terms, and one eight-year term for crimes of murder, rape, kidnapping, and aggravated assault. Thereafter, he was found guilty of rape of an adult woman, a capital crime under Georgia law. In a separate sentencing proceeding, a jury found that two aggravating circumstances justified capital punishment for Coker's most recent rape conviction: first, the rape occurred during the commission of another capital felony, armed robbery; second, Coker had a prior conviction for a capital felony. On appeal, the Georgia Supreme Court affirmed the death sentence over the claim that it constituted cruel and unusual punishment proscribed by the Eighth Amendment.

Question: Does the Eighth Amendment proscribe the punishment of death for the crime of rape in all circumstances?

Decision: Yes. Plurality opinion by Justice White. Vote: 7–2, Powell, Brennan, and Marshall concurring, Burger and Rehnquist dissenting.

Reasons: The Eighth Amendment prohibits criminal sentences that are "grossly disproportionate" to the severity of the crime. Application of this test requires consideration of "public attitudes concerning a particular sentence—history and precedent, legislative attitudes, and the response of juries reflected in their sentencing decisions are to be consulted."

The nation today no longer accepts death as a penalty for the rape of an adult woman. At present, Georgia is the only state that authorizes such punishment, in contrast to the eighteen states that did so in 1925. In addition, sentencing juries in Georgia have declined to impose a death sentence for rape in at least nine out of ten cases. These facts, while not controlling, strongly confirm the judgment that capital punishment for the rape of an adult woman is grossly disproportionate. Although the crime of rape is "highly reprehensible," unlike murder it does not cause death. Rape, with or without aggravating circumstances, cannot be punished by death so long as the rapist spares the life of the victim.

Gardner v. *Florida*, 430 U.S. 349 (1977)

Facts: A defendant was convicted of first-degree murder punishable either by life imprisonment or by death. In a separate sentencing hearing, an advisory jury found that mitigating circumstances outweighed aggravating circumstances and recommended that a life sentence be imposed. The trial judge rejected the recommendation and imposed the death penalty, relying in part on factual information contained in a presentence report that was not disclosed to the defendant or his counsel. The defendant sought review of his sentence on the theory that due process prohibited the imposition of capital punishment on the basis of information that he had no opportunity to deny or explain.

Question: Did the trial judge's partial reliance on the undisclosed presentence report to impose capital punishment violate due process?

Decision: Yes. Plurality opinion by Justice Stevens. Vote: 7–2, Burger, White, and Blackmun concurring, Marshall and Rehnquist dissenting.

Reasons: The landmark decision of *Williams* v. *New York*, 337 U.S. 241 (1949), established the general principle that confidential information obtained in a presentence investigation may be used by a judge in imposing sentence without violating due process. The death sentence, however, is unique in its finality, and the procedures leading to its imposition must therefore be circumscribed by stringent due process safeguards.

The state offers several arguments to justify application of the *Williams* principle to the death penalty. First, it is claimed that confidentiality of presentence reports is required to obtain accurate and candid information concerning the character and background of a defendant. Although this interest is weighty, confidential information may also be unreliable. That unreliability frequently can be detected only if the information is disclosed to the defendant. At least when death is at stake, the interest in reliability outweighs the interest in confidentiality.

The state also claims that disclosure of presentence reports will delay the sentencing proceeding unduly because of disputes over their accuracy. However, the sentencing judge can avoid delay by disregarding any disputed material; if the disputed material is of critical importance, the time invested in ascertaining the truth is constitutionally justified when it makes the difference between life and death.

Finally, it is asserted that judges can be trusted to exercise their sentencing discretion responsibly on the basis of secret information. But *Furman* v. *Georgia*, 408 U.S. 238 (1972), forecloses the claim that judges may impose the death sentence without clear and articulated standards. The participation of defense counsel in the sentencing process in capital cases, moreover, may be critical to a proper evaluation of the relevance and significance of aggravating and mitigating facts.

Accordingly, the defendant was denied due process "when the death sentence was imposed, at least in part, on the basis of information which he had no opportunity to deny or explain."

Dobbert v. *Florida*, 432 U.S. 282 (1977)

Facts: Decided on June 22, 1972, *Furman* v. *Georgia*, 408 U.S. 238, held unconstitutional a Georgia statute giving jurors uncontrolled discretion in determining whether to impose the death sentence in capital cases. On July 17, 1972, the Florida Supreme Court held that *Furman* required invalidation of a state statute requiring the death penalty for capital felonies unless a majority of the jury recommended otherwise. Florida enacted a new death penalty statute in late 1972 that requires extensive procedural safeguards for sentencing in capital cases, and the constitutionality of that statute was upheld in *Proffitt* v. *Florida*, 428 U.S. 242 (1976). Dobbert was convicted and sentenced to death under the 1972 statute for brutally murdering two of his children. The murders occurred before the *Furman* decision and before the enactment of the 1972 statute. In affirming the death sentence, the Florida Supreme Court rejected the claims that the constitutional prohibition against ex post facto laws and the commands of the equal protection clause barred application of the 1972 death penalty procedures to murders committed before their enactment.

Question: Did retroactive application of death penalty procedures enacted in Florida in 1972 violate either the ex post facto or equal protection clauses of the U.S. Constitution?

Decision: No. Opinion by Justice Rehnquist. Vote: 6–3, Brennan, Marshall, and Stevens dissenting.

Reasons: Article I, section 10, of the Constitution prohibits a state from passing any ex post facto law. A law is ex post facto if it makes criminal an act that when committed was innocent, or aggravates the punishment for a crime after its commission, or retroactively changes the quantum of proof necessary to convict. But mere procedural changes in the criminal law, even if disadvantageous to a particular defendant, are not ex post facto. Here the questioned 1972 statute altered only the procedures necessary to impose a death sentence. It did not aggravate the punishment for murder, raise the quantum of proof needed to convict, or make criminal homicides that when committed were innocent.

In addition, the 1972 law provides greater procedural protections than existed in Florida under the earlier death-penalty statute. For the imposition of capital punishment it requires a separate sentencing hearing in which any aggravating and mitigating circumstance can be presented, an advisory jury verdict, and written findings by the sentencing judge showing that specified aggravating factors outweigh mitigating factors.

Death sentences, moreover, are automatically reviewed by the Florida Supreme Court and will be overturned if inconsistent with sentences imposed in similar cases. In Dobbert's case, the advisory jury recommended leniency, which would have prevented capital punishment under the earlier death penalty law. But "viewing the totality of the procedural changes wrought by the new statute, we conclude that [it] did not work an onerous application of an *ex post facto* change in the law."

It is argued that when Dobbert murdered his children, Florida lacked a "valid" death penalty statute because of its subsequent invalidation after *Furman*. Thus, it is claimed, the 1972 statute made criminal what formerly was innocent. But the invalidated statute provided Dobbert with fair warning "of the penalty which Florida would seek to impose on him if he were convicted of first-degree murder. This was sufficient compliance with the *ex post facto* provision of the United States Constitution."

The equal protection clause is also advanced as a barrier to the death sentence imposed upon Dobbert. After *Furman*, the Florida Supreme Court commuted to life imprisonment all death sentences imposed under the invalidated statute. Since Dobbert's crimes were likewise committed before the invalidation, it is claimed that equal protection entitles him to the same treatment as those whose sentences were commuted. But unlike those prisoners, Dobbert was neither tried nor sentenced prior to *Furman*.

> Florida obviously had to draw the line at some point between those whose cases which had progressed sufficiently far in the legal process so as to be governed solely by the old statute, with the concomitant unconstitutionality of its death penalty provision, and those whose involving acts which could properly be subjected to punishment under the new statute. There is nothing irrational about Florida's decision to relegate petitioner to the latter class, since the new statute was in effect at the time of his trial and sentence.

Brown v. Ohio, 432 U.S. 161 (1977)

Facts: In November 1973, Brown stole a car located in East Cleveland, Ohio. In December, he was caught driving the car in Wickliffe, Ohio, and convicted of the crime of joy riding—taking or operating a car without the owner's consent. Thereafter, Brown pleaded guilty to a charge of auto theft brought by Cuyahoga County authorities. He sought unsuccessfully to withdraw his plea on the ground that the charge was barred by the Fifth Amendment protection against double jeopardy. An Ohio appellate court held that the offense of joy riding was a lesser offense included in that of automobile theft. The former offense required proof of all elements of the latter offense, except for an intent to deprive the car owner of his property permanently. The court asserted, however, that Brown's two prosecutions stemmed from separate acts occurring in November and December. Thus, it reasoned, the charge of automobile theft was not tantamount to a constitutionally prohibited second prosecution for joy riding.

Question: Did the charge of automobile theft violate the double jeopardy clause of the Fifth Amendment?

Decision: Yes. Opinion by Justice Powell. Vote: 6–3, Burger, Blackmun, and Rehnquist dissenting.

Reasons: The double jeopardy clause prohibits multiple prosecutions for the same offense. *Blockburger* v. *United States*, 284 U.S. 299 (1932), established the test for determining whether two offenses are the same for double jeopardy purposes: identity exists unless each offense requires proof of a fact which the other does not. Here every element of the offense of joy riding is included in the offense of automobile theft. The offenses are thus the same and trigger protection against double jeopardy, whatever the sequence in which a defendant is prosecuted.

Protection against double jeopardy did not lapse simply because the prosecutions for joy riding and theft were focused on acts occurring in different months. This is because Ohio statutes make the theft and operation of a single car a single offense. "Accordingly, the specification of different dates in the two charges on which Brown was convicted cannot alter the fact that he was placed twice in jeopardy for the same offense in violation of the Fifth Amendment."

United States v. Martin Linen Supply Co., 430 U.S. 564 (1977)

Facts: A federal district court discharged a deadlocked jury in a criminal contempt prosecution against two corporations. Thereafter, pursuant to Rule 29(c) of the Federal Rules of Criminal Procedure, the district court entered judgments of acquittal after finding insufficient evidence of criminal contempt. The court of appeals declined to entertain an appeal by the government on the ground that a retrial would violate the double jeopardy clause of the Fifth Amendment.

Question: Was the appeal by the government barred because a retrial of the corporate defendants after the entry of judgments of acquittal would violate the double jeopardy clause?

Decision: Yes. Opinion by Justice Brennan. Vote: 7–1, Burger dissenting. Rehnquist did not participate.

Reasons: Under the Criminal Appeals Act of 1970, the government is authorized to appeal in criminal cases except where an appeal is barred by the double jeopardy clause. The clause protects against the threat of multiple prosecutions, but offers no immunity from government appeals where a new trial would not be required. Thus, in *United States* v. *Wilson*, 420 U.S. 332 (1975), the Court held that a postverdict dismissal of an indictment after a verdict of guilty could be appealed because restoration of the verdict, not a new trial, would necessarily result if the government prevailed.

In this case, however, judgments of acquittal were entered under Rule 29(c) and terminated a trial in which jeopardy had attached to the criminal defendants. The acquittals were not based on technicalities but on the insufficiency of the evidence. It is a fundamental rule of double jeopardy jurisprudence that a verdict of acquittal, whether based on error or otherwise, cannot be appealed.

Lee v. United States, 432 U.S. 23 (1977)

Facts: Charged with the crime of theft in an information, Lee requested a bench trial. After the opening statement by the prosecution, he moved to dismiss the information for failing to allege knowledge or intent, an element of the crime charged. With the defendant's consent, the district court deferred ruling on the belated motion until the trial was completed. It then dismissed the information for the reason advanced by Lee, despite evidence establishing his guilt beyond any reasonable doubt. Thereafter, Lee was indicted and convicted of theft. The court of appeals rejected his claim that the second trial was barred by the double jeopardy clause of the Fifth Amendment.

Question: Was the second trial of Lee for theft barred by the double jeopardy clause?

Decision: No. Opinion by Justice Powell. Vote: 8–1, Marshall dissenting.

Reasons: United States v. *Jenkins,* 420 U.S. 358 (1975), held that the double jeopardy clause prohibits reprosecution after an initial prosecution has terminated in the defendant's favor by an order contemplating an end to all prosecution. Here a defective information, not doubts of Lee's guilt, aborted the initial trial. In addition, the dismissal order contemplated a second prosecution. *Jenkins* thus did not bar retrial of Lee.

Because the dismissal was tantamount to a declaration of mistrial and was granted at Lee's request, a retrial was constitutionally permissible. *United States* v. *Dinitz,* 424 U.S. 600 (1976), established the general rule that where a mistrial is declared at the defendant's request the double jeopardy clause ordinarily raises no barrier to reprosecution. A retrial is barred, however, where a mistrial is triggered by judicial or prosecutorial error and is committed in bad faith or to harass or prejudice the defendant. In this case, neither the failure of the prosecution to draft the information correctly nor the deferred ruling by the district court on Lee's motion to dismiss was the product of any misconduct. Under the *Dinitz* rule, therefore, retrial of Lee was constitutional.

Jeffers v. United States, 432 U.S. 137 (1977)

Facts: A federal grand jury returned two indictments against Jeffers. The first alleged that Jeffers and nine others violated 21 U.S. Code 846 by conspiring to distribute heroin and cocaine. The second charged that Jeffers alone violated 21 U.S. Code 848 by acting in concert with and as leader of five or more persons to distribute heroin and cocaine. Jeffers successfully opposed a motion by the government to try both the section 846 and section 848 charges together. Thereafter, he and six codefendants were convicted of the section 846 conspiracy charge. Jeffers then moved to dismiss the section 848 indictment on the ground that it placed him in jeopardy for the same offense charged in the section 846 trial in violation of the Fifth Amendment. The motion was denied, Jeffers was convicted, and the court of appeals upheld the conviction.

Question: Was the section 848 prosecution against Jeffers barred by the double jeopardy clause of the Fifth Amendment?

Decision: No. Plurality opinion by Justice Blackmun. Vote: 5–4, White concurring, Stevens, Brennan, Stewart, and Marshall dissenting.

Reasons: The double jeopardy clause generally protects against multiple prosecutions for the same offense. Two offenses are identical for this purpose unless each requires proof of a fact which the other does not. Here all the elements of a section 846 conspiracy offense are included in a section 848 acting-in-concert offense, which also requires proof of a leadership role in the crime. Accordingly, the offenses are the same because section 846 is a lesser included offense of section 848.

In *Brown v. Ohio*, 432 U.S. 161 (1977), the Court established a general rule that protection against double jeopardy prohibits the prosecution of a defendant for the greater offense after he has been convicted of a lesser included offense. But that protection cannot be asserted by a defendant, such as Jeffers, who successfully objects to a trial of the greater and lesser offenses in a single proceeding. Here Jeffers was solely responsible for the successive section 846 and section 848 prosecutions. "Under the circumstances, we hold that his action deprived him of any right that he might have had against consecutive trials."

Lefkowitz v. Cunningham, 431 U.S. 801 (1977)

Facts: A New York statute divests the officer of a political party of his position and imposes a five-year disqualification from holding any other party or public office if he refuses to waive the Fifth Amendment privilege against self-incrimination when the conduct of his office is under investigation. These sanctions were triggered when the chairman of the state Democratic Committee of New York refused to waive his privilege before a grand jury. The chairman obtained a federal district court order enjoining enforcement of the statute on the ground that it violated his Fifth Amendment rights.

Question: Does the challenged statute violate the Fifth Amendment by penalizing the exercise of the privilege against self-incrimination?

Decision: Yes. Opinion by Chief Justice Burger. Vote: 7–1, Stevens dissenting. Rehnquist did not participate.

Reasons: Garrity v. *New Jersey*, 385 U.S. 493 (1967), and its progeny established the principle that the "government cannot penalize assertion of the constitutional privilege against compelled self-incrimination by imposing sanctions to compel testimony that has not been immunized." Here the questioned statute penalizes invocation of the privilege by the officer of a party in several ways. It reduces his political influence and professional reputation, eliminates the perquisites of office, and raises a five-year barrier to prospective party or public offices. The ouster from office in a party, moreover, infringes a person's freedom of political association, which is protected by the First Amendment.

The state has a compelling interest in preserving public confidence in the integrity of the political process. By granting use immunity from criminal prosecution, the state can compel an officer of a party to account for wrongdoing associated with his office. Absent this protection, a state cannot justify coercing citizens to incriminate themselves simply because such incrimination serves a need of the government.

United States v. *Washington*, 431 U.S. 181 (1977)

Facts: A person suspected of theft was called before a grand jury and interrogated without being informed that he was a target of its investigation. The suspect was, however, advised in the grand jury room of his Fifth Amendment privilege against compulsory self-incrimination. After choosing to answer questions, the suspect was indicted for grand larceny and receiving stolen property. He moved to suppress his testimony and quash the indictment on the ground that it was based on evidence obtained in violation of his Fifth Amendment privilege. The trial court granted the motion, holding that the accused had not effectively waived his Fifth Amendment rights because he lacked understanding of their significance. The court of appeals affirmed the suppression order, adding that the Fifth Amendment entitled the accused to be informed that he was a target of investigation by a grand jury and to be advised of his Fifth Amendment rights outside the cloister of the grand jury.

Question: Did the interrogation of the suspect by the grand jury violate his Fifth Amendment privilege against compulsory self-incrimination?

Decision: No. Opinion by Chief Justice Burger. Vote: 7–2, Brennan and Marshall dissenting.

Reasons: The Fifth Amendment protects only against compulsory self-incrimination. The test of compulsion is "whether, considering the totality of circumstances, the free will of the witness was overborne." Here the suspect was explicitly advised of his Fifth Amendment right to remain silent and that any statements he made could be used against him in a criminal prosecution. These warnings removed any possible coercive effects of the grand jury environment which might otherwise cause witnesses to incriminate themselves. Thus, the suspect's answers to questions of the grand jury were not compelled.

The failure to inform a suspect that he is a target of investigation by a grand jury is irrelevant to the compulsion test. "Because target witness status neither enlarges nor diminishes the constitutional protection against compelled self-incrimination, potential defendant warnings add nothing of value to protection of Fifth Amendment rights." The Court added that there is no constitutional vice in advising witnesses of their Fifth Amendment rights in the cloister of the grand jury.

Brewer v. *Williams*, 430 U.S. 387 (1977)

Facts: Arrested and arraigned for kidnapping in Davenport, Iowa, Williams was instructed over the telephone by his attorney in Des Moines to say nothing to the police. It was agreed between the attorney and the Des Moines police that they would drive to Davenport and bring Williams to Des Moines without interrogating him during the trip. Before the Davenport–Des Moines drive commenced, Williams was advised by another attorney not to make any statements without first consulting counsel, and the police agreed again not to question Williams during the journey. With knowledge that Williams was a former mental patient and deeply religious, a detective elicited incriminating statements during the trip to Des Moines by

41

playing on Williams's sympathies for the parents of the kidnapped victim. At his trial for first-degree murder, Williams unsuccessfully sought to suppress the statements and related evidence on the ground that they were obtained in violation of his Sixth Amendment right to counsel. The conviction of Williams was overturned in federal habeas corpus proceedings on the ground that the trial court erred in failing to uphold his Sixth Amendment claim.

Question: Were Williams's incriminating statements obtained in violation of his Sixth Amendment right to counsel?

Decision: Yes. Opinion by Justice Stewart. Vote: 5–4, Burger, White, Blackmun, and Rehnquist dissenting.

Reasons: In *Kirby* v. *Illinois*, 406 U.S. 682 (1972), the Court held that an accused has a right to the assistance of counsel at or after the time that judicial proceedings have been initiated against him—"whether by way of formal charge, preliminary hearing, indictment, information, or arraignment." Williams thus had a right to counsel during the trip to Des Moines. It was admitted that the detective's conversations with Williams were intended to elicit incriminating information and were thus tantamount to interrogation. The case is thus governed by the rule of *Massiah* v. *United States*, 377 U.S. 201 (1964), "that once adversary proceedings have commenced against an individual, he has a right to legal representation when the government interrogates him."

The conviction of Williams can be upheld only if he waived his right to counsel during the interrogation that occurred on the trip to Des Moines. To prove waiver of the right to counsel, the state must show that the defendant knew of that right and that he relinquished or abandoned it intentionally. Such proof was lacking here. Williams was advised twice by attorneys to remain silent during the trip and knew of the agreements by the police not to interrogate him. He was nevertheless interrogated without being informed of his right to the presence of an attorney and without any inquiry as to whether he wished to waive that right. The record in this case provides no reasonable basis for finding a waiver.

Weatherford v. *Bursey,* 429 U.S. 545 (1977)

Facts: A state undercover agent participated with Bursey and others in vandalizing a Selective Service office. After informing the police of the incident, the agent was arrested and charged along with

Bursey in order to maintain his capability of performing other undercover work.

In preparing for trial, Bursey and his attorney requested and held meetings with the agent on two occasions in order to discuss defense strategy. The agent, acting in good faith, denied that he would testify against Bursey and transmitted no information or plans discussed at the meetings to the prosecuting attorney. On the day of Bursey's trial, the government decided to call the agent as a witness for the prosecution because he had apparently lost his cover. The testimony of the agent did not include any information derived from the meetings with Bursey and his counsel. After conviction, Bursey sued the undercover agent and his superior for damages under 42 U.S. Code 1983. He alleged that participation by the agent in the pretrial meetings violated his Sixth Amendment right to effective assistance of counsel and his right to a fair trial, which is protected by the due process clause.

The district court found for the defendants. The court of appeals reversed, holding that the Sixth Amendment prohibits the prosecution from knowingly permitting an agent to intrude into the attorney-client relationship. In addition, it concluded that the failure to reveal the identity of the agent before trial and the error of the agent in stating he would not testify for the prosecution interfered with Bursey's preparation for trial in violation of due process.

Question: Was Bursey denied his constitutional rights to effective assistance of counsel and a fair trial by the activities and use of the undercover agent in securing his conviction?

Decision: No. Opinion by Justice White. Vote: 7–2, Brennan and Marshall dissenting.

Reasons: In this case, there is no evidence that participation by the agent in conversations with Bursey and his counsel prejudiced Bursey's defense. The record shows that the prosecution neither used the agent to testify about the conversations nor otherwise derived any evidence or benefit from the agent's presence at the pretrial meetings. In addition, the agent participated only at Bursey's request and for the purpose of maintaining his undercover capability, not to spy.

> There being no tainted evidence in this case, no communication of defense strategy to the prosecution, and no purposeful intrusion by [the agent], there was no violation of the Sixth Amendment. . . . We [do not] believe that federal or state prosecutors will be so prone to lie or the difficulties

of proof so great that we must always assume not only that an informant communicates what he learns from an encounter with the defendant and his counsel but also that what he communicates has the potential for detriment or benefit to the prosecutor's case.

Bursey's right to a fair trial was not violated by the pretrial concealment of the agent's identity and his denial that he would testify against Bursey. "There is no general constitutional right to discovery in a criminal case." The prosecution was thus under no duty to reveal the names of its witnesses prior to trial. The agent's misrepresentation that he would not testify for the prosecution, moreover, was unintentional. And there is no claim that the belated decision to call the agent as a witness substantially prejudiced the defense in its cross-examination. The use of a surprise witness or unexpected evidence does not violate a defendant's right to a fair trial.

Marks v. *United States*, 430 U.S. 188 (1977)

Facts: Several defendants were prosecuted for transporting obscene material in interstate commerce in violation of 18 U.S. Code 1465. The alleged crime occurred before the Supreme Court expanded the constitutional definition of obscenity in *Miller* v. *California*, 413 U.S. 15 (1973). At trial, the district court denied the request of the defendants for jury instructions under the pre-*Miller* standards of obscenity enunciated in *Memoirs* v. *Massachusetts*, 383 U.S. 413 (1966).[21] After conviction, the defendants appealed, claiming that retroactive application of *Miller* to conduct that was innocent under the prior obscenity standards enunciated in *Memoirs* violated due process.

Question: Does the due process clause of the Fifth Amendment prohibit retroactive application of *Miller* in a criminal case to reach conduct that was constitutionally protected from punishment at the time of its commission under the prevailing views of the Supreme Court?

Decision: Yes. Opinion by Justice Powell. Vote 9–0.

Reasons: The due process clause guarantees a right to fair warning that particular conduct may trigger criminal penalties. This right

---

[21] Under *Memoirs*, expressive material could not be obscene unless it was "utterly without redeeming social value." Under *Miller*, material may be obscene if it lacks "serious literary, artistic, political, or scientific value."

is protected against both legislative and judicial action. In *Bouie* v. *City of Columbia*, 378 U.S. 347 (1964), the Court held that an unforeseen enlargement of a state criminal trespass statute applied retroactively violated due process. Similarly, *Memoirs* marked the bounds of obscenity prior to *Miller* and protected expressive materials unless they were "utterly without redeeming social value." *Miller* represented a significant departure from *Memoirs* and expanded the permissible scope of obscenity laws to reach materials lacking "serious literary, artistic, political or scientific value." The defendants in this case had no fair warning that their questionable conduct would be subject to the new *Miller* obscenity standards. "We therefore hold . . . that the Due Process Clause precludes the application to [defendants] of the standards announced in *Miller* v. *California*, to the extent that those standards may impose criminal liability for conduct not punishable under *Memoirs*." The Court also concluded that the defendants could invoke the protection of any constitutional principle enunciated in *Miller* favorable to their defense.

Smith v. United States, 431 U.S. 291 (1977)

Facts: Smith was indicted and tried for mailing obscene materials to adults in violation of federal law (18 U.S. Code 1461). The mailings occurred wholly within Iowa, during a time when Iowa permitted the distribution of obscene material to adults. Smith moved for a directed verdict of acquittal on the theory that the obscenity laws of Iowa established the applicable community standard for determining whether materials were obscene. Thus, he contended, the mailing of materials that offended no state law was not proscribed by section 1461. Denying the motion, the district court instructed the jury that contemporary community standards for purposes of determining obscenity under federal law are set by what is in fact accepted by the local community as a whole. In making that determination, the jurors were permitted to draw on their own knowledge of the average person in the community, state obscenity law, and the types of materials available for purchase. After conviction, Smith appealed, claiming that the district court erred in its interpretation of section 1461.

Question: Does section 1461 permit jurors to draw on their own knowledge of community standards and to depart from community standards reflected in state obscenity laws in determining whether material is obscene?

Decision: Yes. Opinion by Justice Blackmun. Vote: 5–4, Brennan, Stewart, Marshall, and Stevens dissenting.

Reasons: In *Hamling* v. *United States*, 418 U.S. 87 (1974), the Court held that section 1461 embraced the three-part constitutional definition of obscenity adopted in *Miller* v. *California*, 413 U.S. 15 (1973):

> (a) whether "the average person, applying contemporary community standards" would find that the work, taken as a whole, appeals to the prurient interest . . . ; (b) whether the work depicts or describes, in a patently offensive way, sexual conduct specifically defined by the applicable [federal] law, and (c) whether the work, taken as a whole, lacks serious literary, artistic, political or scientific value.

Hamling also held that section 1461 required the use of local rather than national community standards in determining whether materials appeal to the prurient interest and are patently offensive. It would be both inappropriate and virtually impossible for a legislature to define local community standards in these regards. "Contemporary community standards must be applied by juries in accordance with their own understanding of the tolerance of the average person in their community." Although local or state obscenity laws are relevant evidence of community mores, in federal obscenity prosecutions under section 1461 they are not conclusive on the question of what community standards tolerate.

Abortion and Contraceptives

The 1973 decision of the Supreme Court recognizing a woman's constitutional right to an abortion free from state interference[22] has spawned sharp political controversy. Several proposed constitutional amendments have been introduced in Congress that would narrowly circumscribe a woman's right to an abortion.[23] In addition, the issue of whether federal Medicaid funds should be used to subsidize abortion for indigents has provoked heated controversy within Congress and considerable lobbying by proabortion and antiabortion groups. This term, in a trio of decisions bitterly condemned by proabortion groups, the Court held that states were not required by

---

[22] Roe v. Wade, 410 U.S. 113 (1973).

[23] See, for example, S. J. Res. 6, 95th Congress, 1st session (1977). Section 1 of the resolution provides: "With respect to the right to life guaranteed in this Constitution, every human being, subject to the jurisdiction of the United States, or of any State, shall be deemed, from the moment of fertilization, to be a person and entitled to the right to life."

either federal statute or the Constitution to subsidize elective abortions as a condition to the receipt of Medicaid funds (*Beal* v. *Doe,* 432 U.S. 438 [1977]; *Maher* v. *Roe,* 432 U.S. 464 [1977]) and could prohibit nontherapeutic abortions at publicly owned hospitals (*Poelker* v. *Doe,* 432 U.S. 519 [1977]).

Many cited these decisions as illustrative of the inexcusable failure of the Court to embrace the constitutional claims of politically weak minorities in order to provide shelter from the hazards of the majoritarian political process. By throwing the question of whether government should subsidize abortions into the political arena, some said, the Court equated the constitutional rights of minorities with the wishes of unthinking legislatures that would ignore the self-evident social and economic costs of unwanted children.

These criticisms of the Court's abortion decisions are misguided for several reasons. First, the laws that were sustained provided subsidies for "medically necessary" but not elective abortions. Medical necessity was broadly defined to include preservation of the mother's mental or physical health. It would be a gross exaggeration to characterize such laws as the product of majoritarian excesses.[24]

Second, proabortionists have in the past exhibited powerful political clout. This dispels the view that they are doomed to legislative failure. Before the decisions of the Supreme Court in *Roe* v. *Wade*[25] and *Doe* v. *Bolton,*[26] which recognized a constitutional right to abortion, proabortionists had successfully lobbied several state legislatures to relax restrictions on abortions.[27] Their 1973 victories in the Court, however, seemed to engender a political ennui among their constituents and apparently enervated organizational and educational campaigns supportive of abortions. In contrast, the antiabortionists rallied their forces after *Roe* v. *Wade* and succeeded in pushing antiabortion legislation through Congress,[28] garnering a majority of popular support against subsidized abortions.[29] The

---

[24] Despite the decision of the Court, sixteen states continued voluntarily to provide funds for elective abortions for indigents. See *Washington Post*, November 17, 1977. Many indigents may be able to obtain privately financed abortions because of their modest cost, generally in the neighborhood of $150.

[25] 410 U.S. 113 (1973).

[26] 410 U.S. 179 (1973).

[27] 410 U.S. at 140, n. 37.

[28] Section 209 of P.L. 94-439 prohibited the use of federal Medicaid funds to pay for abortions for fiscal 1977 "except where the life of the mother would be endangered if the fetus were carried to term."

[29] A recent *New York Times*–CBS poll found that the public opposed government-subsidized abortions by a margin of 55 percent to 38 percent. See *New York Times*, July 29, 1977.

political weakening of proabortionist groups after *Roe* v. *Wade* dramatically illustrates the injury done to democratic processes when the Supreme Court moves to remove an issue of fundamental public concern from the political branches by pronouncing its resolution through constitutional mandate.

Third, issues related to abortion involve attitudes about human life and death, and the treatment by any community of questions pertaining to abortion will reflect a mixture of religious, scientific, ethical, and other values. Whether to prohibit, discourage, permit, or encourage abortion will depend in large measure on necessarily tentative views of the community as to the nature and meaning of life. These unanswerable questions are especially appropriate for legislative rather than constitutional resolution. In recognition that "time has upset many fighting faiths," the Supreme Court should be most reluctant to discover permanent answers to the unanswerable mysteries of conception and death in the Constitution.[30]

The three decisions of the Supreme Court concerning abortion failed to resolve all constitutional issues relating to Medicaid funding of abortions. The Court specifically reserved decision on whether funding that failed to subsidize all medically necessary abortions would pass constitutional muster. The reasoning of *Maher* v. *Roe* strongly suggests an affirmative answer. The issue will undoubtedly be raised in court challenges to a federal appropriations statute that narrowly limits the use of Medicaid funds for abortions.[31]

In contrast to abortion, the use of contraceptives is apparently viewed as socially and morally acceptable by most people. In *Carey* v. *Population Services International*, 431 U.S. 678 (1977), the Court held that the constitutional right of privacy embraces the choice by an adult of obtaining contraceptives. In striking down a law limiting the distribution of contraceptives to licensed pharmacists, the Court concluded that only a compelling state interest could justify restrictions on the marketing of such devices to adults.

Population Services also invalidated a wholesale ban on the distribution of contraceptives to minors under the age of sixteen, bringing applause from those concerned about the approximately

---

[30] See Abrams v. United States, 250 U.S. 616, 630 (1919) (Holmes, J., dissenting).
[31] See P.L. 95-205, 95th Congress, 1st session (1977). This statute prohibits the use of federal funds to pay for abortions unless continued pregnancy would endanger the mother's life or, in the opinion of two doctors, cause the woman to suffer severe and long-lasting physical damage to her health. The legislation also appropriates funds for "medical procedures" to treat victims of rape or incest if the offenses have been promptly reported to police or to a public health agency.

1 million teenage pregnancies annually.[32] There was no evidence to support the view that teenage sexual promiscuity was affected by the availability of contraceptives, and, in the absence of such proof, the Court ruled that a state cannot obstruct the right of minors to obtain contraceptives.

Finally, *Population Services* held that a blanket prohibition on the advertising of contraceptive devices ran afoul of the First Amendment. This does not necessarily presage advertisement of contraceptives on radio or television, because the First Amendment tolerates reasonable restrictions on free speech that limit the time, place, and manner of its exercise.[33]

Beal v. *Doe*, 432 U.S. 438 (1977)

Facts: Title XIX of the Social Security Act, 42 U.S. Code 1396 et seq., establishes a medical assistance program (Medicaid) that provides federal funds to participating states. To qualify for federal funds, a state must provide financial assistance to needy persons for five general categories of medical treatment. A qualifying state is not required to fund all medical treatment falling within these categories, but its Medicaid plan must have "reasonable standards . . . for determining . . . the extent of medical assistance under the plan which . . . are consistent with the objectives of [Title XIX]." Pennsylvania's federally approved Medicaid plan provided financial assistance for abortions necessary to protect the mental or physical health of the mother but denied assistance for nontherapeutic abortions. A federal court of appeals held that Title XIX required Pennsylvania's Medicaid plan to fund the costs of all abortions during the first and second trimesters of pregnancy.

Question: Does Title XIX require states participating in the Medicaid program to finance the costs of both medically necessary and nontherapeutic abortions for needy individuals?

Decision: No. Opinion by Justice Powell. Vote: 6–3, Blackmun, Brennan, and Marshall dissenting.

---

[32] See U.S. Department of Health, Education and Welfare, National Center for Health Statistics, *Vital Statistics Report*, vol. 25, no. 10 (December 30, 1976); U.S. Department of Health, Education and Welfare, Center for Disease Control, *Abortion Surveillance* (1975), fig. 3, p. 41.

[33] See Cox v. New Hampshire, 312 U.S. 569 (1941); compare Red Lion Broadcasting Co. v. FCC, 395 U.S. 367 (1969).

Reasons: A state Medicaid plan satisfies the coverage requirements of Title XIX if it has reasonable standards for determining the extent of medical assistance offered that are consistent with the primary objective of the Medicaid program—to assist needy persons in obtaining necessary medical services. The refusal of a state to fund unnecessary abortions neither undermines this objective nor is unreasonable. Although the Pennsylvania plan provides assistance for the greater expenses associated with childbirth, that is a reasonable choice, because the state has a "strong and legitimate interest in encouraging normal childbirth."

Maher v. Roe, 432 U.S. 464 (1977)

Facts: By regulation, Connecticut limits state Medicaid benefits for abortions during the first trimester of pregnancy to those that are necessary to preserve the mental or physical health of the mother. The regulation also provides Medicaid benefits for childbirth. Denied state financial assistance for nontherapeutic abortions, indigent mothers brought suit in federal district court, claiming that the regulation violated the equal protection clause of the Fourteenth Amendment. The district court held that the equal protection clause forbids a state welfare program from subsidizing childbirth and medically necessary abortions but not elective abortions.

Question: Does the equal protection clause require a state welfare program to subsidize nontherapeutic abortions if it pays for childbirth and medically necessary abortions?

Decision: No. Opinion by Justice Powell. Vote: 6–3, Blackmun, Brennan, and Marshall dissenting.

Reasons: Unless it discriminates against a suspect class or burdens a fundamental right, a state law passes muster under the equal protection clause if it rationally relates to a legitimate state interest. Here the questioned regulation discriminates against indigent women seeking abortions, but financial need alone does not make a class suspect for equal protection purposes. In addition, the regulation does not burden a woman's fundamental right, recognized in *Roe v. Wade*, 410 U.S. 113 (1973), to obtain an abortion during the first trimester of pregnancy. That right prevents a state from interfering with the abortion decision; it does not limit a state's power to favor childbirth over abortion in the allocation of public funds. The contested regulation makes childbirth a financially more attractive choice for indigent women than elective abortions, but it erects no additional barrier to the obtaining of abortions. Accordingly, the regulation survives equal protection scrutiny if it has a rational basis.

A state has a strong and legitimate interest in protecting the potential life of the fetus and encouraging childbirth. Subsidizing the substantial medical costs associated with childbirth is a rational means of advancing this interest.

> We certainly are not unsympathetic to the plight of an indigent woman who desires an abortion . . . [but] the decision whether to expend state funds for nontherapeutic abortions is fraught with judgments of policy and value over which opinions are sharply divided. . . . The appropriate forum for [resolving such sensitive issues] in a democracy is the legislature.

The Constitution does not proscribe government funding of nontherapeutic abortions. Congress may require such funding as a condition of participation by a state in the federally subsidized Medicaid program, but the Constitution does not require government subsidies for nontherapeutic abortions simply because subsidies are provided for childbirth.

In a related case, *Poelker v. Doe*, 432 U.S. 519 (1977), the Court enlisted the reasoning of *Maher* to uphold the authority of publicly owned hospitals to provide services to indigents for childbirth without providing corresponding services for nontherapeutic abortions.

Carey v. Population Services International, 431 U.S. 678 (1977)

Facts: A New York statute makes it a crime for any person to sell or distribute a contraceptive to a person under the age of sixteen, for any person except a licensed pharmacist to distribute contraceptives to persons over the age of sixteen, and for anyone to advertise or display contraceptives. A federal district court held the entire statute unconstitutional. It concluded that the right of privacy protects the decision whether or not to beget children and that the restrictions on the sale and distribution of contraceptives unconstitutionally interfered with such decisions. In addition, it concluded that the blanket prohibition on advertising contraceptive devices violated the First Amendment protection of free speech.

Question: Are the criminal prohibitions of New York on the sale, distribution, and advertising of contraceptives unconstitutional?

Decision: Yes. Plurality opinion by Justice Brennan. Vote: 7–2, White, Powell, and Stevens concurring, Burger and Rehnquist dissenting.

Reasons: The constitutional right of privacy protects the interest of an individual in making certain kinds of decisions regarding marriage, procreation, contraception, family relationships, and child rearing. Government interference with these private decisions can be sustained only if it is justified by a compelling countervailing interest.

Here the challenged statute interferes with decisions whether or not to beget children by restricting the sale and distribution of contraceptives. Persons over sixteen can obtain contraceptives only through licensed pharmacists. This restriction lessens the availability of contraceptives and reduces the opportunity for privacy of selection and purchase. Moreover, legitimate state interests in quality control of contraceptive devices and the protection of young employees from exposure to contraceptive products are not advanced by the restriction. Thus, giving licensed pharmacists a monopoly over the distribution of contraceptives to persons over sixteen unconstitutionally burdens the right of privacy.

The wholesale ban on the distribution of contraceptives to persons under the age of sixteen suffers from a similar constitutional defect. Having less capability of making important decisions than adults and traditionally subject to greater state control, minors can be prohibited from obtaining contraceptives if the prohibition serves "any significant state interest." New York claims that the blanket prohibition advances its significant interest in discouraging sexual promiscuity among minors. Nothing in the record supports the view that the incidence of sexual activity among minors is related to the availability of contraceptives, however.

> When a State, as here, burdens the exercise of a fundamental right, its attempt to justify that burden as a rational means for the accomplishment of some significant state policy requires more than a bare assertion, based on a conceded absence of supporting evidence, that the burden is connected to such a policy.

Finally, the complete prohibition on the advertisement or display of contraceptives must fall under First Amendment scrutiny. In *Virginia State Board of Pharmacy* v. *Virginia Citizens Consumer Council*, 425 U.S. 748 (1976), the Court held that a state is constitutionally barred from totally suppressing truthful commercial speech relating to lawful activity. Merely because the advertisement of contraceptive products might offend or embarrass some does not justify a departure from this rule. It is well established that free speech cannot be suppressed merely because of hostility that may be aroused by its exercise.

Freedom of Speech, Press, and the Establishment of Religion

In a decision that rocked the legal world and sent ripples through other professions, the Court struck down a state law that prohibited truthful advertising of routine legal services in newspapers (*Bates* v. *State Bar of Arizona*, 433 U.S. 350 [1977]). The opinion of the Court added significant new dimensions to the doctrine of commercial speech under the First Amendment, while leaving many questions unanswered.

That truthful commercial advertisements are protected by the First Amendment was unequivocally established in *Bigelow* v. *Virginia*, 421 U.S. 809 (1975). There the Court concluded that state prohibitions against truthful advertising survive First Amendment attack only if they advance legitimate government interests that outweigh the public interest in disseminating the information. In *Virginia State Board of Pharmacy* v. *Virginia Citizens Consumer Council*, 425 U.S. 748 (1976), the Court invalidated a state ban on advertising the prices of prescription drugs. It found a strong public interest in the commercial advertisement of prices, because advertising serves to promote efficiency in a free market economy. In contrast, it concluded that any paternalistic interest the state might have had in suppressing price information to prevent consumers from unwisely relying on prices in making drug purchases collided with the underlying premises of the First Amendment and was thus wholly illegitimate.

Bates carried the reasoning of *Virginia State Board of Pharmacy* to the professions. It found that any state interest in maintaining professional dignity, preventing a deterioration in services, or avoiding enforcement problems was insufficient to outweigh the significant public interest in truthful price advertising by lawyers. The claim was rejected that advertising the price of any type of legal service was inherently misleading. Although the holding of *Bates* applies only to newspaper advertising by lawyers, its reasoning would condemn a broad range of prohibitions imposed on advertising by practitioners of a number of professions, such as doctors, architects, engineers, and accountants. By promoting price competition and expanding the knowledge of consumers about legal services, *Bates* will probably expedite the current trends toward greater specialization and use of paraprofessionals in the delivery of services. This might put a damper on the persistent inflation that at present plagues the service sector of the economy.[34] A New York City divorce lawyer has stated that lawyers' fees for uncontested divorces fell from $750 to between $150 and $250 in the wake of *Bates*.[35]

Bates left open several important questions, the resolution of which will determine whether it was a frontal assault or a peripheral attack on barriers to advertising by professionals. The Court opined that advertising the quality of services might be so inherently misleading as to justify total suppression, that problems of radio or television advertising might justify special restrictions, and that ignorance on the part of consumers might justify certain warnings or disclaimers in professional advertising. Whether abuses in advertising occur under the limited umbrella of *Bates* will bear heavily on the approach of the Court to these issues.

Commercial speech received the constitutional blessing of the First Amendment in two other decisions this term. In *Linmark Associates, Inc. v. Willingboro*, 431 U.S. 85 (1977), the Court condemned the attempt by a municipality to curb flight of white homeowners from a racially integrated community by prohibiting the posting of *For Sale* or *Sold* signs on all but model homes. Likewise, a wholesale ban by New York on the advertisement of contraceptives failed to pass First Amendment scrutiny in *Carey v. Population Services International*, 431 U.S. 678 (1977).

One aspect of free speech is the right to refrain from speaking. The scope of that constitutional protection was addressed twice this term and produced a significant victory for unions of public employees.[36] At issue in *Abood v. Detroit Board of Education*, 431 U.S. 209 (1977), was whether public employees could refuse to pay service fees tantamount to union dues because of their ideological opposition to collective bargaining in the public sector. The gist of the claim under the First Amendment was that mandatory payment compelled support of collective bargaining and thus coerced support of political positions the claimants opposed. Although acknowledging the validity of the claim, the Court found that a countervailing interest in promoting collective-bargaining arrangements and pre-

[34] See U.S. Office of Management and Budget, *1977 Economic Report of the President*, Table B-49.

[35] "Lawyer Advertising Issue Preoccupies ABA Delegates," *Washington Post*, August 12, 1977.

[36] Of approximately 11.5 million civilian public employees, about 2.6 million belong to public or professional associations.

venting "free riders" from profiting from union activities justified the infringement of free speech. On the other hand, the Court found no constitutional justification for compelling public employees to contribute to union activities unrelated to collective bargaining.

In the light of *Abood*, a decision by federal, state, or local governments to permit so-called agency-shop arrangements with their unions is of increased significance to public employees. In *Madison Joint School District* v. *Wisconsin Employment Relations Commission*, 429 U.S. 167 (1976), the Court unanimously condemned a union's quest to prevent nonunion teachers from speaking against an agency shop during public school-board meetings.

In the second "refraining from speech" case (*Wooley* v. *Maynard*, 430 U.S. 705 [1977]), the Court sustained the right of a Jehovah's witness to obscure a state motto on his motor vehicle license plates because of opposition to its ideological message, "Live Free or Die."

The First Amendment bars Congress and the states from making laws "respecting an establishment of religion." As construed by the Court, the establishment clause does not command a hermetic seal between church and state; rather, it raises only a blurry barrier that seems indistinct even to the most clairvoyant. The financial difficulties of church-related schools have prompted several states to offer various forms of government aid to the schools and their students and parents. Since 1971, the Court has addressed the constitutionality of several such aid programs.[37] Although adopting a single three-pronged test[38] by which to determine whether government aid to church-related schools violates the establishment clause, the Court has applied the standard inconsistently, with a bewildering variety of results.[39] The ad hoc approach of the Court to establish-

---

[37] See Lemon v. Kurtzman, 403 U.S. 602 (1971).

[38] To pass constitutional muster under the establishment clause, the aid must have a secular purpose, have a principal primary effect that neither advances nor inhibits religion, and avoid fostering an excessive entanglement between government and religion.

[39] Compare, for example, Lemon v. Kurtzman, 403 U.S. 602 (1971) (invalidating state reimbursement of teachers' salaries and textbooks), Committee for Public Education and Religious Liberty v. Nyquist, 13 U.S. 756 (1973) (invalidating tuition reimbursements, income tax benefits, and grants for maintenance and repair of school facilities), and Meek v. Pittenger, 421 U.S. 349 (1975) (invalidating the provision of "auxiliary services" and the loan of instructional materials and equipment to students), with Tilton v. Richardson, 403 U.S. 672 (1971) (upholding construction grants for buildings and facilities used solely for educational purposes), Board of Education v. Allen, 392 U.S. 236 (1968) (upholding loan of textbooks to students), and Roemer v. Board of Public Works, 426 U.S. 736 (1976) (upholding noncategorical grants to church-related colleges).

ment-clause issues encourages legislatures to seek ways around their latest decisions, perhaps encouraging political divisions along religious lines that the clause was meant to forestall. The constitutional waters of establishment-clause litigation remained muddied and meandering after a badly divided Court decided *Wolman* v. *Walter*, 433 U.S. 229 (1977). The plurality opinion by Justice Blackmun received but two of nine votes. It concluded that Ohio could provide nonpublic school pupils with books, standardized testing and scoring, diagnostic services, and therapeutic services. It found a bar under the establishment clause, however, to the provision of instructional materials and equipment for classroom use and of transportation for field trips. The failure of *Wolman* to supply cogent and consistent reasoning [40] in distinguishing between constitutionally permissible and constitutionally defective aid promises to beget a new round of challenges under the establishment clause with uncertain results.

A "human cannonball" act provided a bizarre setting for the Court's only significant free press case during this term. The core dispute was over money. At a county fair, a television broadcaster filmed an entertainer's entire fifteen-second act during which he was shot from a cannonball into a net. The entire performance was later broadcast on an evening news program. Suing for damages, the entertainer claimed that the broadcast violated his common law right of publicity. In *Zacchini* v. *Scripps-Howard Broadcasting Co.*, 433 U.S. 562 (1977), the Court rejected by a narrow margin of five to four, the broadcaster's attempt to advance a First Amendment shield to bar the damage suit. The practical implications of the decision are difficult to decipher because it was narrowly restricted to the broadcasting of a performer's entire act.

Bates v. *State Bar of Arizona*, 433 U.S. 350 (1977)

Facts: The Supreme Court of Arizona suspended two attorneys from the practice of law for advertising their legal services in contravention of a disciplinary rule. Placed in a newspaper, the legal advertisement stated that the attorneys operated a legal clinic and charged "very reasonable" fees. It listed their prices for legal services that would be provided in connection with certain routine

---

[40] Out of apparent desperation, the Court has brought a minimum degree of certainty to litigation under the establishment clause by mechanically invoking the doctrine of *stare decisis* to uphold (loan of textbooks) or condemn (loan of instructional materials and equipment) particular types of state aid although the results are not logically reconcilable. See Wolman v. Walter, 433 U.S. 229, at 251, n. 18 (1977).

matters: uncontested divorces, uncontested adoptions, simple personal bankruptcies, and changes of name. A disciplinary rule issued by the state supreme court generally proscribed advertising by lawyers, with limited exceptions. The suspended attorneys unsuccessfully claimed that the disciplinary rule was preempted by the Sherman Act because it restricted competition and violated their First Amendment rights of free speech.

Questions: (1) Does the broad disciplinary rule of Arizona against legal advertising violate the Sherman Act? (2) As applied to prohibit truthful advertising in newspapers about routine legal services, does the rule violate the First Amendment?

Decision: No to the first question and yes to the second. Opinion by Justice Blackmun. Vote: 9–0 on the first question and 5–4 on the second, Burger, Rehnquist, Powell, and Stewart dissenting.

Reason: In *Parker* v. *Brown*, 317 U.S. 341 (1943), the Court held that state officials acting at the command of a state statute were immune from suit under the Sherman Act. The so-called state action immunity afforded by *Parker* rests on the premise that state laws having anticompetitive effects are not automatically preempted by the act.

Here a rule issued by a state supreme court is contested. As part of a disciplinary code to protect the public, it forbids legal advertising and is actively enforced by the state. These facts, coupled with the traditional and significant interest of states in regulating lawyers, entitle the disciplinary rule to the *Parker* v. *Brown* shelter from the Sherman Act.

The First Amendment claim turns largely on the decision in *Virginia State Board of Pharmacy* v. *Virginia Consumer Council*, 425 U.S. 748 (1976). There the Court invalidated a state statute prohibiting pharmacists from advertising the prices of prescription drugs. It noted that truthful commercial speech is entitled to First Amendment protection unless outweighed by countervailing state interests. *Virginia State Board of Pharmacy* also concluded that the First Amendment prohibits states from banning truthful commercial advertising for the purpose of protecting consumers from unwise choices.

At issue here is a newspaper advertisement of routine legal services. Six countervailing state interests are said to justify its proscription.

First, it is argued that legal advertising will degrade and tarnish the image of the legal profession. This assertion is questionable, since other professionals, such as bankers and engineers, have advertised without loss of dignity. It is recognized by all that attorneys offer services for profit. Advertising fees for routine legal services reflects this reality and assists consumers in searching for legal advice. Its speculative effects on professional dignity do not outweigh its First Amendment virtues.

Second, it is claimed that all legal advertising is misleading. While advertising of unique or specialized legal services may be inherently misleading, prices for routine services can be advertised without deception. Routine services generally require the same work for each client and can be offered at standardized rates. Although the quality of service may vary, this possibility accompanies virtually all advertising. "If the naiveté of the public will cause advertising by lawyers to be misleading, then it is the bar's role to assure that the populace is sufficiently informed as to enable it to place advertising in its proper perspective."

Third, it is asserted that legal advertising will cause more litigation. There is no legitimate interest, however, in raising barriers to a person's redress of a legal wrong. A majority of the population underutilizes attorneys because of ignorance of legal problems and the cost of legal services. Legal advertising can reduce this ignorance to the benefit of the bar and consumers.

Fourth, it is claimed that legal advertising will increase the price of legal services and entrench the market power of established lawyers. Neither argument is persuasive or relevant to the First Amendment issue. Legal advertising may reduce prices by increasing competition and spurring productivity. It also offers new lawyers a ready means of challenging the market position of established attorneys.

Fifth, it is argued that advertising prices will reduce the quality of legal services by encouraging attorneys to cut corners. Restraints on advertising, however, are a clumsy and ineffective way to fight shoddy legal work, and advertising the prices of routine legal services may improve quality by standardizing the procedures for handling certain problems of clients.

Sixth, it is argued that a wholesale ban on advertising is necessary because restraining only false or deceptive advertising would create difficult enforcement problems. This argument is premised on the erroneous view that the legal profession will abuse the opportunity for advertising. "For every attorney who over-reaches . . . there will be thousands of others who will be candid and honest and straightforward." Difficulties of enforcement do not justify the suppression of all advertising by attorneys.

Finally, the particular advertisement at issue is claimed to be misleading and thus constitutionally unprotected in three respects: its use of the undefined phrase "legal clinic," its description of fees as "very reasonable," and its failure to state that changes of name can be obtained without the services of an attorney. The term *legal clinic* was not misleading because the public generally understands it to mean a business offering standardized and multiple legal services. The advertised fees were in fact at the lower end of the market range and thus could fairly be described as very reasonable. Most legal services can be performed by consumers for themselves, and the failure to disclose that fact in legal advertising is not inherently misleading. Accordingly, the contested advertising of routine legal services was protected by the First Amendment.

The Court noted that its decision leaves open the degree of constitutional protection afforded legal advertising about the quality of service and its dissemination through radio, television, or personal solicitation. It emphasized the fact that "because the public lacks sophistication concerning legal services, misstatements that might be overlooked or deemed unimportant in other contexts may be found quite inappropriate in legal advertising."

Linmark Associates, Inc. v. *Willingboro*, 431 U.S. 85 (1977)

Facts: To prevent "white flight" and panic selling of homes when its racial composition was in flux, a municipality passed an ordinance prohibiting the posting of *For Sale* or *Sold* signs on all but model homes. Finding the fears of the municipality unjustified, a federal district court invalidated the ordinance as a violation of the First Amendment protection of free speech. The court of appeals reversed.

Question: Does the First Amendment prohibit a municipality from suppressing *For Sale* or *Sold* signs on homes in order to prevent the flight of white homeowners from a racially integrated community?

Decision: Yes. Opinion by Justice Marshall. Vote: 8–0. Rehnquist did not participate.

Reasons: Bigelow v. *Virginia*, 421 U.S. 809 (1975), established the proposition that truthful commercial speech is protected by the First Amendment. Its suppression can be justified only if necessary to advance strong and legitimate state interests. To promote stable, racially integrated housing, the contested ordinance forbids the posting of *For Sale* or *Sold* signs because of the commercial message they convey. The ordinance is constitutionally defective for two reasons. First, the record failed to show that the suppressed signs were in fact causing white flight and panic selling. Second, the First Amendment forbids the suppression of truthful commercial speech for the purpose of preventing prospective recipients from acting in ways the government believes would conflict with their self-interests. The constitutionally permissible remedy for such perceived problems is more speech, not enforced silence. Here a fear that homeowners would act unwisely after seeing *For Sale* and *Sold* signs prompted adoption of the ordinance. The First Amendment cannot tolerate such a paternalistic approach to governing.

Abood v. *Detroit Board of Education*, 431 U.S. 209 (1977)

Facts: Michigan law authorizes collective bargaining between unions of public employees and local government employers and permits agency-shop arrangements. These arrangements require every employee represented by a union—whether the employee is a member of the union or not—to pay a service fee, equal in amount to union dues, as a condition of employment. A teachers' union and a board of education concluded a collective-bargaining agreement providing for an agency shop. Nonunion teachers brought suit in state court challenging the constitutionality of the agency shop under the First Amendment. On account of their opposition to collective bargaining in the public sector and to political causes supported by the union, the teachers claimed that the mandatory service fee violated their rights to refrain from supporting these activities. A state appellate court denied the nonunion teachers any relief.

Questions: (1) Does an agency-shop arrangement involving public employees violate the First Amendment rights of nonunion employees who oppose collective bargaining in the public sector? (2) Does an agency-shop arrangement involving public employees violate the First Amendment insofar as it permits union expenditures of service fees for political and ideological purposes unrelated to collective bargaining and opposed by nonunion employees who paid the fees?

Decision: No to the first question and yes to the second. Opinion by Justice Stewart. Vote: 9–0.

Reasons: An agency-shop arrangement advances the strong interest of the government in having a fair and effective collective-bargaining system where a freely elected union is the exclusive representative of all employees within its jurisdiction. In the process of negotiating and administrating a collective-bargaining agreement, a union must expend time and money in obtaining the services of lawyers, economists, researchers, and other types of personnel. An agency shop "has been thought to distribute fairly the cost of these activities among those who benefit, and it counteracts the incentive that employees might otherwise have to become free riders—to refuse to contribute to the union while obtaining benefits of union representation that necessarily accrue to all employees."

The agency shop may compel employees to support collective-bargaining activities that they oppose on political, religious, or other grounds. For example, a union might negotiate a wage policy or a medical-benefits plan covering abortions to which an employee has political or ideological objection. But, at least in the private sector, *Railway Employes Department* v. *Hanson*, 351 U.S. 225 (1956), and *International Association of Machinists* v. *Street*, 367 U.S. 740 (1961), concluded that the large contribution agency shops make to a fair and effective system of collective bargaining justifies their intrusion on First Amendment interests stemming from the bargaining activities and tactics of a union. The balance of constitutional interests struck in *Hanson* and *Street* should not be overturned simply because public-sector bargaining is involved. One may concede that public-sector bargaining is more political than private-sector bargaining, because decisions made by a public employer are part of the political process.

> Whether [public officials] acede to a union's demands will depend upon a blend of political ingredients, including community sentiment about unionism generally and the involved union in particular, the degree of taxpayer resistance, and the views of voters as to the importance of the service involved and the relation between the demands and the quality of service.
>
> It is surely arguable . . . that permitting public employees to unionize and a union to bargain as their exclusive representative gives the employees more influence in the decisionmaking process than is possessed by employees similarly organized in the private sector.

But the political nature of public-sector bargaining does not confer greater First Amendment rights on public employees than on similarly situated private employees. Both can be compelled financially to support union activities incident to collective bargaining that conflict with their beliefs. Agency shops in the public sector pass constitutional muster insofar as "service charges are applied to collective bargaining, contract administration, and grievance adjustment purposes."

The First Amendment, however, bars a union from spending part of a nonmember's service fee over his objection to contribute to political causes or to express political views unrelated to its bargaining duties. This agency-shop practice is tantamount to compelling an individual to support political goals and ideas he opposes as a condition of public employment. The First Amendment protects the right of an individual to decline to make contributions for political purposes, and the government may not make forfeiture of this right a condition of employment. Accordingly, a teachers' union may not require nonmembers "to contribute to the support of an ideological cause [they] may oppose as a condition of holding a job as a public school teacher." A nonmember who generally expresses objection to ideological expenditures of any sort unrelated to collective bargaining is entitled to a remedy providing for a refund of the proportion of his service fees spent for such purposes and a reduction of future service fees by the same proportion.

Madison Joint School District v. *Wisconsin Employment Relations Commission*, 429 U.S. 167 (1976)

Facts: During collective-bargaining negotiations with a teachers' union, a local school board held a public meeting devoted in part to expression of opinion by the public. Over the union's objection, the board permitted a nonunion teacher to express opposition to any agency-shop agreement that would require nonunion teachers to pay union dues. The union filed a complaint against the school board with the Wisconsin Employment Relations Commission, claiming that permitting nonunion teachers to speak on a subject of current collective-bargaining negotiations was an unlawful labor practice. The commission, in upholding the claim, ordered the board to deny all but union representatives permission to speak on collective-bargaining subjects during public meetings. Rejecting the contention of the board that the order unconstitutionally infringed freedom of speech, the Supreme Court of Wisconsin affirmed.

Question: Did the finding by the commission of an unlawful labor practice and its remedial order violate the First Amendment protection of free speech?

Decision: Yes. Opinion by Chief Justice Burger. Vote: 9–0.

Reasons: The order of the commission substantially restricted the First Amendment rights of nonunion teachers to express their views to the school board on matters subject to collective bargaining. The asserted justification for the restriction is its contribution to effective collective bargaining. Assuming the validity of that justification, the finding of an unfair labor practice was not based on proof that the teacher's presentation created a clear and present danger to collective bargaining. He spoke at a public meeting as an employee and a concerned citizen, but not as a legally recognized bargaining representative.

> The participation in public discussion of public business cannot be confined to one category of interested individuals. To permit one side of a debatable public question to have a monopoly in expressing its views to the government is the antithesis of constitutional guarantees. . . . When the board sits in public meetings to conduct public business, it may not be required to discriminate between speakers on the basis of their employment, or the content of their speech.

The finding by the commission of an unlawful labor practice thus violated the First Amendment. Its remedial order forbidding the board to permit future public discussion by nonunion speakers on issues subject to collective bargaining is also constitutionally defective. The order constitutes an unjustified prior restraint on free speech.

Wooley v. Maynard, 430 U.S. 705 (1977)

Facts: A New Hampshire statute requires noncommercial vehicles to bear license plates embossed with the state motto, "Live Free or Die." Another New Hampshire statute makes it a crime to obscure the motto. A member of the Jehovah's Witnesses sect was convicted three times for covering up the state motto on his automobile license plates. He disagreed with the motto on moral, religious, and political grounds and objected to disseminating its message by displaying the motto on his automobiles. Threatened with additional prosecutions, the follower and his wife obtained a federal district court injunction forbidding their arrest or prosecution for obscuring the state motto. The district court held that the First Amendment prohibited a state from punishing this conduct.

Question: May a state constitutionally require an individual to participate in the dissemination of an ideological message by displaying it on his private property in a manner and for the express purpose that it be observed and read by the public?

Decision: No. Opinion by Chief Justice Burger. Vote 7–2, Rehnquist and Blackmun dissenting.

Reasons: The First Amendment protects both the right to speak freely and the right to refrain from speaking. In *West Virginia State Board of Education* v. *Barnette*, 319 U.S. 624 (1943), the Court held that the First Amendment protected a public school student's choice to decline to participate in daily public ceremonies honoring the flag both with words and gestures. In this case, the contested New Hampshire statutes require individuals to use their private property as a mobile billboard to foster an ideological message—"Live Free or Die." "The First Amendment protects the rights of individuals . . . to refuse to foster, in the way New Hampshire commands, an idea they find morally objectionable."

No strong countervailing state interest justifies invasion by New Hampshire of this First Amendment protection. The state claims that requiring the display of the state motto on license plates facilitates the identification of passenger vehicles and promotes a particular type of appreciation of history, individualism, and state pride. There are alternative means of readily identifying passenger vehicles that do not stifle First Amendment freedoms, however, and "where the State's interest is to disseminate an ideology . . . such interest cannot outweigh an individual's First Amendment right to avoid becoming the courier for such message."

Zacchini v. *Scripps-Howard Broadcasting Co.*, 433 U.S. 562 (1977)

Facts: Zacchini, an entertainer, is shot from a cannon into a net during his fifteen-second "human cannonball" act. During Zacchini's performance at an Ohio county fair, a broadcasting company filmed his entire act and later broadcast it on an evening news program. Zacchini sued the broadcaster for damages, alleging that the unauthorized showing of his performance violated his right to publicity protected by Ohio common law. While acknowledging a right of publicity, the Ohio Supreme Court rejected Zacchini's damage claim. It reasoned that the First Amendment shields a broadcaster from damages for televising entertainment of legitimate public interest in its newscasts where there is no intent to injure a particular entertainer.

Question: Does the First Amendment protect broadcasters from damage suits based on the broadcast of an entertainer's entire act in violation of a state-recognized right of publicity?

Decision: No. Opinion by Justice White. Vote: 5–4, Powell, Brennan, Marshall, and Stevens dissenting.

Reasons: Zacchini's damage claim stems from the broadcast of his entire performance, alleged to be an appropriation of his professional property. A state has a legitimate interest in protecting such proprietary interests to encourage public entertainment. That protection, of course, would not prevent the reporting of newsworthy facts about the human cannonball act. But, at the same time, "wherever the line in particular situations is to be drawn between media reports that are protected and those that are not, we are quite sure that the First and Fourteenth Amendments do not immunize the media when they broadcast a performer's entire act without his consent."

This rule is necessary to prevent the unjust enrichment of broadcasters at the expense of entertainers and to provide the latter with an economic incentive to produce performances of public interest.

Wolman v. *Walter,* 433 U.S. 229 (1977)

Facts: An Ohio statute authorizes the state to provide pupils in nonpublic schools with books, instructional materials and equipment, standardized testing and scoring, diagnostic services, therapeutic services, and transportation for field trips. The initial biennial appropriation for implementation of the statute was $88 million. To qualify for state aid, a pupil must attend a nonpublic school that admits students and hires teachers without regard to religious creed.

Ohio taxpayers brought suit attacking the constitutionality of the statute on the ground that it violated the establishment clause of the First Amendment. The litigants stipulated that more than 96 percent of nonpublic school students in Ohio attended sectarian schools and more than 92 percent attended Catholic schools. It was also stipulated that a majority of teachers in Catholic schools were members of the Roman Catholic faith and that Christian symbols decorated many rooms and hallways. A federal district court sustained the constitutionality of the contested state aid in all its forms, despite its conclusion that one purpose of the church-related schools was the inculcation of religious doctrine.

Question: Do the various types of state aid that Ohio provides to nonpublic schools and pupils violate the establishment clause of the First Amendment?

Decision: No, except for the provision of instructional materials and equipment to students and the expenditures for field trip transportation. Plurality opinion by Justice Blackmun. Vote: 6–3, Burger, White, Rehnquist, and Powell voting to uphold, and Brennan, Marshall, and Stevens voting to condemn virtually all the state aid.

Reasons: A statute that provides aid to church-related schools passes muster under the establishment clause if it passes a three-part test: "[It] must have a secular legislative purpose, must have a principal or primary effect that neither advances nor inhibits religion, and must not foster an excessive government entanglement with religion." This test creates only a "blurred, indistinct, and variable barrier" between church and state.

The questioned statute satisfies the first prong of the test, because its purposes are to protect student health and to assist the secular education of all school children. The several types of state aid, however, fare differently under the effect and entanglement prongs.

• *Textbooks.* The statute authorizes the loan of secular textbooks, approved for use in public schools, to students in nonpublic schools at their request. This type of state aid was sustained in *Board of Education* v. *Allen*, 392 U.S. 236 (1968), and *Meek* v. *Pittenger*, 421 U.S. 349 (1975), and the Court declined to overrule those decisions.

• *Testing and scoring.* Nonpublic schools are provided standardized tests and scoring services to measure the progress of students in secular subjects. Personnel of nonpublic schools are involved neither in drafting nor in scoring the tests, nor are they paid for the costs of administration of the tests. The testing and scoring services enable nonpublic schools to ensure that their students are receiving an adequate secular education and create no threat of diversion for religious purposes. State provision of the services is thus constitutional.

• *Diagnostic services.* Public health employees offer speech, hearing, and psychological diagnostic services within nonpublic schools. *Lemon* v. *Kurtzman*, 403 U.S. 602 (1971), concluded that states may provide church-related schools with secular or nonideological services, such as bus transportation or public health services, without offending the establishment clause. The diagnostic services at issue here pass constitutional scrutiny under this standard. They have little or no educational content and provide virtually no opportunity for advancing religious views.

- *Therapeutic services.* Public employees provide certain therapeutic, career counseling, and remedial services to nonpublic school pupils needing specialized attention. Depending on convenience, the services are provided in public schools, public centers, or mobile units located off the premises of nonpublic schools. Unlike the diagnostician, the therapist may establish a relationship with a pupil that creates an opportunity for transmitting religious views. But this danger is minimal when the therapist is a public employee and works in a neutral site off the premises of nonpublic schools. Accordingly, the provision of therapeutic services will neither advance religion impermissibly nor require excessive government surveillance to ensure this result. It is thus constitutional.

- *Instructional materials and equipment.* Pupils in nonpublic schools are lent materials and equipment such as projectors, tape recorders, globes, and science kits. *Meek* v. *Pittenger* invalidated a direct loan of state materials and equipment to nonpublic schools. There the Court reasoned that since the schools are devoted largely to inculcating religious beliefs, the use of instructional materials and equipment in the classroom would inevitably advance a religious enterprise. This reasoning is equally applicable when materials and equipment are lent to pupils for use in nonpublic school classrooms. The Ohio program for lending instructional materials and equipment is thus unconstitutional.

- *Field trips.* To enrich secular studies, transportation services for field trips are supplied to pupils in nonpublic schools for visits to government, industrial, cultural, and scientific centers. Teachers in nonpublic schools select the time, frequency, and destination of the trips. In addition, the teacher gives the field trip its educational value by discussing the place to be visited and by guiding the activities and thoughts of students during the trip. Because teachers in nonpublic schools seek to inculcate religious beliefs, state funding of field trips, under the rationale of *Meek*, advances religion unconstitutionally. Moreover, excessive government entanglement with religion would result from the type of state supervision of nonpublic teachers that would be necessary to ensure that only secular use of field trip funds was made.

Mt. Healthy City Board of Education v. *Doyle*, 429 U.S. 274 (1977)

Facts: A school teacher was refused re-employment, owing in part to his having informed a radio station of a memorandum that his principal had circulated concerning the dress and appearance of teachers. Claiming that the refusal violated his First Amendment right of free speech, the teacher successfully sued the school board in federal district court and obtained a judgment ordering reinstatement and back pay. The district court found that the teacher's constitutionally protected communication to the radio station played a "substantial part" in the decision to deny re-employment. It also found that the teacher had committed acts of misconduct that would have justified a refusal to renew his contract for valid reasons. But, because a constitutionally impermissible reason contributed substantially to the re-employment decision, the district court ruled that reinstatement and back pay were constitutionally required remedies. It rejected the board's assertion that the Eleventh Amendment immunized it from suit.

Questions: (1) Was the school board immune from suit under the Eleventh Amendment? (2) Does the First Amendment require the reinstatement and back pay of a government employee simply because exercise of First Amendment rights played a substantial part in a decision to refuse to renew his contract?

Decision: No to both questions. Opinion by Justice Rehnquist for a unanimous Court.

Reasons: Generally speaking, the Eleventh Amendment forbids federal courts from entertaining damage suits against a state without its consent. It offers no protection to political subdivisions or municipal corporations, however. Since the school board in this case is substantially independent from state control, it cannot be considered an arm of the state and thus entitled to any immunity under the Eleventh Amendment.

> Regarding the merits, the defect in the district court's rule is that it would require reinstatement in cases where a dramatic and perhaps abrasive incident [protected by the First Amendment] is inevitably on the minds of those responsible for the decision to rehire, and does indeed play a part in that decision—even if the same decision would have been reached had the incident not occurred. The constitutional principle at stake is sufficiently vindicated if such an employee is placed in no worse a position than if he had not engaged in the conduct.

Accordingly, even if a government employee has shown that his constitutionally protected conduct was a "motivating factor" in a decision to deny employment, reinstatement is not required if the government shows by a preponderance of the evidence that the same decision would have been made if the conduct had never occurred. The case was remanded to determine whether the school board had valid reasons for denying the teacher re-employment under this test.

Civil Rights and Civil Liberties

Doctrinal crosscurrents characterized the treatment by the Court of civil rights and civil liberties. It pushed on two fronts to expand the protections offered by the due process and equal protection clauses of the Fourteenth Amendment. In *Moore* v. *City of East Cleveland, Ohio*, 431 U.S. 494 (1977), a plurality opinion by Justice Powell revived the doctrine of substantive due process in invalidating a housing ordinance that barred a grandmother from residing with two grandsons. Matters relating to family life, the Court reasoned, enjoy a strong due process shield that can be pierced only by important government interests. A 1963 decision[41] of the Warren Court had sapped the vitality of substantive due process. Its resuscitation this term to protect the home of a grandmother refutes assertions that civil liberties are mechanically balanced away by the Burger Court.

In addition, in *Trimble* v. *Gordon*, 430 U.S. 762 (1977), the Court granted special equal protection status to illegitimates in striking down a statute denying them intestacy rights upon the death of their fathers. Although illegitimacy is not a "suspect" classification that triggers strict judicial scrutiny, the Court nevertheless applied a heightened level of equal protection review because discrimination against illegitimates encroaches on fundamental personal rights. At present, the Court has enunciated four distinct levels of equal protection scrutiny depending on the classification at issue.[42] The com-

---

[41] Ferguson v. Skrupa, 372 U.S. 726 (1963).

[42] Classifications based on race, ancestry, or alienage (when drawn by a state) trigger a compelling government interest test, at least where benign discrimination is not at issue (Hunter v. Erickson, 393 U.S. 385 [1969]; Graham v. Richardson, 403 U.S. 365 [1971]; Casteneda v. Partida, 430 U.S. 482 [1977]). Classifications based on sex satisfy equal protection scrutiny only if substantially related to the achievement of important government objectives (Craig v. Boren, 429 U.S. 190 [1976]). Trimble v. Gordon requires heightened equal protection review of classifications based on illegitimacy. Other classifications generally hurdle equal protection commands if they are rationally related to advancing a legitimate government interest (Massachusetts Board of Retirement v. Murgia, 427 U.S. 307 [1976]).

plexity that this adds to equal protection analysis may push the Court to adopt a more candid ad hoc balancing test in all equal protection cases.[43]

In contrast to *Moore* and *Trimble*, the Court was reluctant to offer constitutional protection in five other cases in which civil liberties were at issue. The most controversial of these raised the question of whether the use of corporal punishment to maintain discipline in a school contravened the Eighth Amendment prohibition against cruel and unusual punishment. In *Ingraham* v. *Wright*, 430 U.S. 651 (1977), the Court said it did not, holding that only criminals could invoke Eighth Amendment protections. Most critics of the decision overlooked the refusal of the Court to foreclose the availability of a damage remedy under the due process clause to students arbitrarily punished for reasons unrelated to educational objectives.

The Court also declined an invitation to entangle the Constitution in foster care disputes. In a narrow holding sustaining the constitutionality of procedures for removing foster children from foster parents (*Smith* v. *Organization of Foster Families for Equality and Reform*, 431 U.S. 816 [1977]), a unanimous Court expressed grave doubt as to whether the psychological and emotional attachments between the two are entitled to due process protection.

The rapid growth of computer data banks has spurred widespread legislative and public concern over rights of privacy.[44] In what promises to be a forerunner of similar privacy right cases, the Court confronted the potential threats of data banks in *Whalen* v. *Roe*, 429 U.S. 589 (1977). To stem the growing tide of drug abuse, New York used computer tapes to store information on prescription forms that identified the prescribing physician, the dispensing pharmacy, the drug and dosage, and the name, address, and age of the patient. Emphasizing that public disclosure of the information was a crime and that there had been no improper leaks, the Court unanimously rebuffed the claim of a patient that the mere computer storage of prescription information invaded the constitutional protection of the doctor-patient relationship. *Whalen* intimated, however, that a different result might be required where there is proof that data banks have been improperly used.

---

[43] Justice Marshall has advocated a more candid approach to equal protection jurisprudence. See Massachusetts Board of Retirement v. Murgia, 427 U.S. 307 (1976) (dissenting opinion).

[44] See, for example, Privacy Act of 1974, P.L. 93-579, 93rd Congress, 2d session (1974); Family Educational Rights and Privacy Act of 1974, P.L. 93-380, 93rd Congress, 2d session (1974); *Personal Privacy in an Information Society*, Report of the Privacy Protection Study Commission, 1977.

Finally, the Court rejected two procedural due process claims. In *Dixon* v. *Love*, 431 U.S. 105 (1977), it sustained the automatic suspension or revocation of a driver's license upon conviction of three moving traffic offenses within a twelve-month period. Also, in *Codd* v. *Velger*, 429 U.S. 624 (1977), the Court ruled that no hearing is required for nontenured public employees who are discharged for reasons that stigmatize their reputations but which they concede to be true.

Moore v. *City of East Cleveland, Ohio*, 431 U.S. 494 (1977)

Facts: An East Cleveland housing ordinance limits occupancy of a dwelling unit to members of a single family. *Family* is narrowly defined to include only a few categories of related individuals, and the definition excludes a group consisting of more than one dependent child of the head of a household and the dependent's spouse and children. A violation of the ordinance is a criminal offense. Mrs. Moore occupied a dwelling with her son and two grandsons who were cousins; she then received a notice of violation stating that one of the grandsons was an illegal occupant and was directed to comply with the ordinance. Refusing to comply and declining to seek a zoning variance potentially available in cases of hardship, Moore was convicted. She claimed unsuccessfully that the ordinance invaded the constitutional protection afforded family living arrangements under the due process clause. A state appellate court affirmed the conviction.

Question: Did application of East Cleveland's housing ordinance to prohibit two grandsons from residing with their grandmother violate the substantive due process protection afforded family living arrangements under the Fourteenth Amendment?

Decision: Yes. Plurality opinion by Justice Powell. Vote: 5–4, Stevens concurring, Burger, Rehnquist, Stewart, and White dissenting.

Reasons: When government intrudes on matters related to family life, due process requires close judicial scrutiny of the interests advanced by the intrusion. The East Cleveland housing ordinance "slic[es] deeply into the family itself. . . . On its face it selects certain categories of relatives who may live together and declares that others may not. . . . It makes a crime of a grandmother's choice to live with her grandson in circumstances like those presented here."

This drastic regulation of family living arrangements is said to be justified by the need to prevent overcrowding, excess traffic and parking congestion, and undue financial burdens on the school system. The challenged ordinance bears only a tenuous relation to these goals. It permits many types of large household arrangements where several persons may drive cars and attend public school.

Substantive due process "protects the sanctity of the family . . . because the institution of the family is deeply rooted in this Nation's history and tradition." That tradition embraces the bonds uniting members of the nuclear family, as well as ties to uncles, aunts, cousins, and especially grandparents. "Even if conditions of modern society have brought about a decline in extended family households, they have not erased the accumulated wisdom of civilization, gained over the centuries and honored throughout our history, that supports a larger conception of the family." The East Cleveland housing ordinance tramples on this conception too carelessly to satisfy the substantive due process commands of the Fourteenth Amendment.

Trimble v. *Gordon*, 430 U.S. 762 (1977)

Facts: Illinois probate statutes permit legitimate children to inherit by intestate succession from both parents, but extend the intestacy rights of illegitimate children to inheritance only from their mothers. An Illinois probate court denied an illegitimate daughter any inheritance rights after her father died intestate. He was supporting the daughter at the time of death as required by a paternity order and had openly acknowledged her as his child. The Illinois Supreme Court sustained the denial and rejected the claim that the probate statutes invidiously discriminated against illegitimates in violation of the equal protection clause of the Fourteenth Amendment.

Question: Do the Illinois probate statutes discriminate against illegitimates in violation of the equal protection clause?

Decision: Yes. Opinion by Justice Powell. Vote: 5–4, Burger, Stewart, Blackmun, and Rehnquist dissenting.

Reasons: Although classifications based on illegitimacy are not "suspect" under the equal protection clause, a heightened level of judicial scrutiny is justified, because they encroach on fundamental personal rights. Several arguments are offered to support the discriminatory treatment of illegitimates in the Illinois probate statutes. First, the discrimination is claimed to promote legitimate family relationships. But *Weber* v. *Aetna Casualty & Surety Co.*, 406 U.S. 164 (1972), held it illogical, unjust, and unconstitutional to impose disabilities on the illegitimate child for the purpose of deterring irresponsible acts of parents.

Second, the discrimination is said to advance the substantial interest of the state in establishing an accurate and efficient method of disposing of property at death. Because proving maternal ancestry is easier than proving paternity, the questioned probate statutes reduce the likelihood of spurious claims and avoid the administrative burden of holding lengthy paternity hearings. However, there are

> significant categories of illegitimate children of intestate men [whose] inheritance rights can be recognized without jeopardizing the orderly settlement of estates or the dependability of title to property passing under intestacy laws. . . . Difficulties of proving paternity in some situations do not justify the total statutory disinheritance of illegitimate children whose fathers die intestate.

In this case, for example, the intestate was found to be the father of the illegitimate daughter in a state paternity action prior to death. Illinois thus had no constitutionally sufficient reason for denying her inheritance rights.

Finally, it is asserted that the Illinois probate statutes pass constitutional muster under the authority of *Labine* v. *Vincent*, 401 U.S. 532 (1971). There the Court upheld a statute that barred an illegitimate child from sharing equally with legitimate children in the estate of their father, although he had publicly acknowledged the child before dying intestate. Statements in *Labine* suggested that the statute was sustainable because it created no insurmountable barrier to inheritance by illegitimates through a will. Since Illinois also permits illegitimates to inherit through a will, it is argued that *Labine* provides a constitutional stamp of approval on its intestacy laws. The reasoning of *Labine*, however, is disapproved, because alternative methods of inheritance are irrelevant in determining the constitutionality of intestacy statutes that discriminate against illegitimates.

Ingraham v. *Wright*, 430 U.S. 651 (1977)

Facts: Without an opportunity for a hearing, two Dade County, Florida, junior high school students were paddled by school officials for the purpose of maintaining discipline in the school. For belatedly responding to a teacher's instructions, one student was paddled more than twenty times and suffered injuries requiring his absence from school for eleven days. The other student was paddled several times for minor infractions, on one occasion preventing the full use of his arm for a week. Seeking damages and injunctive relief, the students sued in federal district court, alleging that authorization by Dade County of summary corporal punishment to maintain discipline in schools both inherently and as applied to their misdeeds violated the due process clause of the Fourteenth Amendment and the prohibition against cruel and unusual punishment of the Eighth Amendment. The district court dismissed the suit, and the court of appeals affirmed.

Question: Does summary paddling of students as a means of maintaining discipline in a school violate either procedural due process or the Eighth Amendment?

Decision: No. Opinion by Justice Powell. Vote: 5–4, White, Brennan, Marshall, and Stevens dissenting.

Reasons: The use of corporal punishment in the United States as a means of maintaining school discipline has a long history. At common law, a teacher or administrator is privileged in the use of force reasonably believed necessary for a child's proper control, training, or education. The use of excessive or unreasonable force is unlawful in virtually all states. Moderate corporal punishment in public schools has been authorized by twenty-one of the twenty-three state legislatures that have addressed the problem. The constitutional issues in this case must be approached in the light of this background.

The history of the Eighth Amendment indicates it was designed to protect only criminals from cruel and unusual punishments. Every prior decision of the Court that considered whether a punishment violated the amendment dealt with a criminal punishment. Unlike the prisoner who lives in a relatively closed society cut off from family and friends,

> the schoolchild has little need for the protection of the Eighth Amendment. . . . The public school remains an open institution. Except perhaps when very young, the child is not physically restrained from leaving school during school hours. . . . The openness of the public school and its supervision by the community afford significant safeguards against the kinds of abuses from which the Eighth Amendment protects the prisoner.

Thus, the Eighth Amendment is inapplicable to disciplinary corporal punishment imposed by public school teachers or administrators.

Corporal punishment inflicted for misconduct in public schools, nevertheless, deprives students of a liberty interest protected by the due process clause of the Fourteenth Amendment. The punishment thus must be administered in accord with procedural due process requirements. Those requirements turn on three factors: the nature of the private interest at issue, the risk that the questioned procedures will cause erroneous deprivations of that interest, and the probability that additional or substitute safeguards would reduce the risk, and the state interest at stake, including the avoidance of fiscal and administrative burdens.

The student has a strong interest in avoiding unjustified corporal punishment. Under Florida law, however, that risk is insubstantial. The teacher and the principal must first decide whether punishment is warranted. They are subject to civil and criminal penalties if the punishment is later found to have been excessive. Moreover, the record indicates that in Dade County misuse of corporal punishment is an aberration. "Because paddlings are usually inflicted in response to conduct directly observed by teachers in their presence, the risk that a child will be paddled without cause is typically insignificant."

Finally, the state has a strong interest in avoiding any type of hearing before the infliction of corporal punishment to maintain discipline in schools. Hearings would frequently disrupt the classroom, divert personnel and attention from normal pursuits, and undermine the effectiveness of the punishment. In addition, a constitutionally mandated requirement of notice and a hearing before the infliction of disciplinary corporal punishment would significantly intrude into a primary area of state responsibility.

"We conclude that the Due Process Clause does not require notice and a hearing prior to the imposition of corporal punishment in the public schools, as that practice is authorized and limited by the common law." The Court left open the question of whether the due process clause affords a damage or other remedy to public school students who are punished arbitrarily or for reasons unrelated to educational objectives.

Smith v. Organization of Foster Families for Equality and Reform, 431 U.S. 816 (1977)

Facts: Foster parents brought suit challenging the constitutionality of procedures governing the removal of foster children from foster homes under New York statutes and regulations. A federal district court concluded that the preremoval procedures violated due process. It held that before a foster child could be transferred to a new foster home or returned to his natural parents, he was constitutionally entitled to a hearing at which all concerned parties would have an opportunity to present evidence to the administrator charged with determining the future placement of the child.

Question: Do the challenged procedures governing the removal of foster children from foster homes violate due process by failing to require a preremoval hearing at which the foster parents and other concerned parties may participate?

Decision: No. Opinion by Justice Brennan. Vote: 9–0.

Reasons: The New York system of foster care is intended to provide a temporary family for a child during a period when his natural parents are unable to provide a normal family life. Agencies that administer foster care generally require foster parents to agree to return a foster child upon request or within twenty days of notice from a natural parent. Parental responsibilities under the foster care scheme are divided among the agency, the foster parents, and the natural parents. The agency supervises the conduct of foster parents, who exercise day-to-day supervision of the child. Natural parents retain authority to act with respect to the child on matters of special importance, such as marriage or surgery.

A foster care agency is required by regulation to notify foster parents ten days in advance of any proposed removal of a foster child from their home to a new foster home or to the custody of his natural parents. Foster parents are entitled to a conference with the agency, a statement of reasons for removal of the child, and an opportunity to submit reasons against removal with the assistance of counsel. An official must render a written decision on the removal question within five days, and no removal occurs until that time. In addition, foster parents may request a full trial-like hearing before the child is moved to another foster home, as opposed to the custody of his natural parents. Finally, a foster parent may obtain preremoval judicial review of an agency's decision to remove a child who has been in foster care for eighteen months or more.

The constitutional challenge by the foster parents to these procedural safeguards rests on the assumption that their psychological and emotional attachments to foster children are a type of liberty protected by the due process clause of the Fourteenth Amendment. Prior decisions have established that due process protects certain realms of family life. Foster families, however, unlike natural families, derive their existence from state law and contractual arrangements. Giving constitutional recognition to their rights over a foster child, moreover, necessarily derogates from the constitutional rights of the natural parents. These factors undermine the claim of foster parents to a protected liberty interest in the retention of foster children. But even assuming the validity of that claim, the challenged preremoval procedures satisfy due process.

The dictates of procedural due process turn on three factors: the private interest at stake; the risk of an erroneous deprivation of such interest through the questioned procedures and the probable value of other procedural safeguards; and the government interest at stake, including the avoidance of administrative and fiscal burdens. Here New York provides a conference, and in some circumstances a judicial hearing, before a child is moved to a new foster home or to the custody of his natural parents. In addition, foster parents are entitled to a trial-like hearing after an initial determination by an agency to remove a foster child. The district court found these procedures defective for failing to *require* preremoval hearings and the participation of natural parents. But foster parents who decline to request a conference presumably lack the psychological or emotional interests to be protected by a hearing. And natural parents may be consulted at the preremoval conference in cases in which it is appropriate to determine the wisdom of a proposed removal or transfer. Whatever liberty interests foster parents may have in continued care for a foster child, the contested New York procedures satisfy due process requirements for effectuating a deprivation of those interests.

> We deal here with issues of unusual delicacy, in an area where professional judgments regarding desirable procedures are constantly and rapidly changing. In such a context, restraint is appropriate on the part of courts called upon to adjudicate whether a particular procedural scheme is adequate under the Constitution.

Whalen v. *Roe*, 429 U.S. 589 (1977)

Facts: Concerned that drugs having both legitimate and illegitimate uses were being diverted into unlawful channels, New York passed the Controlled Substances Act, providing for comprehensive regulation of drugs having a potential for abuse. With regard to Schedule II drugs, including opium, cocaine, and amphetamines, the act requires that all prescriptions be prepared in triplicate on an official form by a physician. The form requires identification of the prescribing physician, the dispensing pharmacy, the drug and dosage, and the name, address, and age of the patient. One copy of the completed form is sent to a state agency, where its information is transferred to magnetic tapes for processing by a computer. The computer tapes are securely maintained, and public disclosure of the identity of patients is a crime. Shortly after the act took effect, physicians and patients obtained a federal district court order enjoining its enforcement as applied to the reporting of patients' names and addresses. The district court held that the contested reporting provisions violated the constitutional right of privacy that protects the doctor-patient relationship.

Question: Do the provisions of the act for recording and maintaining the names and addresses of patients obtaining Schedule II drugs pursuant to a doctor's prescription violate the patients' constitutional rights of privacy?

Decision: No. Opinion by Justice Stevens. Vote: 9-0.

Reasons: The district court found the patient-identification provisions objectionable because the state failed to prove that they were necessary to the detection and deterrence of unlawful use of drugs. But lack of necessity is not a constitutional vice. The state could rationally have assumed that the identification requirements might deter potential violators as well as aid in the detection and investigation of specific instances of apparent drug abuse. Rationality is all the Constitution requires to sustain the exercise of a state's police powers, in the absence of infringement of a constitutionally protected right.

The claim of the patients is that the constitutional right of privacy protects their interests in avoiding disclosure of personal matters and in making uncoerced decisions having to do with their personal health. It is argued that the act impairs these interests by failing to require proper security of patient information. This is alleged to cause some persons to decline the use of Schedule II drugs. The record, however, fails to support these fears: there is no evidence that the prohibitions of the act against public disclosure have been administered improperly, and requiring disclosure of patient information to a limited number of state employees "does not automatically amount to an impermissible invasion of privacy." The record does show that some use of Schedule II drugs has been discouraged by the patient identification requirements, but the act allows each patient to decide independently, with the advice of his physician, whether or not to use such drugs. Since the state could ban the use of Schedule II drugs, making an insubstantial infringement of a patient's privacy a condition of their use is constitutionally acceptable:

We hold that neither the immediate nor the threatened impact of the patient identification requirements . . . on either the reputation or the independence of patients for whom Schedule II drugs are medically indicated is sufficient to constitute an invasion of any right or liberty protected by the Fourteenth Amendment.

Dixon v. *Love*, 431 U.S. 105 (1977)

Facts: Illinois law authorizes the automatic suspension or revocation of the licenses of drivers who have been convicted of three moving traffic offenses within a twelve-month period; however, such drivers may obtain restricted permits for commercial use or in cases of hardship. A driver whose license was revoked under the law successfully attacked its constitutionality in federal district court on the ground that due process required a prerevocation evidentiary hearing.

Question: Does the automatic revocation of a driver's license under Illinois law violate due process?

Decision: No. Opinion by Justice Blackmun. Vote: 8–0. Rehnquist did not participate.

Reasons: In *Bell* v. *Burson*, 402 U.S. 535 (1971), the Court held that a driver's license is a property or liberty interest that may be suspended or revoked only in compliance with procedural due process. The requirements of procedural due process depend upon several factors: the private interest at stake; the risk of an erroneous deprivation of such interest as a result of the procedures used and the value of additional safeguards; and the government interest at stake, including the avoidance of fiscal or administrative burdens.

A driver's license is of insufficient importance to require an evidentiary hearing prior to its suspension or revocation, especially when restricted permits remain available in cases of hardship or for commercial use. In addition, the risk of an erroneous deprivation is minimal when revocation is automatically triggered by repeated convictions for moving traffic offenses. Finally, there is a strong government interest in promptly removing unsafe drivers from the roads and in avoiding frivolous prerevocation hearings demanded solely to delay the revocation. Consequently, "we conclude that the public interests present under the circumstances of this case are sufficiently visible and weighty for the State to make its summary initial decision effective without a predecision administrative hearing."

Codd v. *Velger*, 429 U.S. 624 (1977)

Facts: A nontenured New York City policeman brought suit under 42 U.S. Code 1983, alleging that without a hearing he had been discharged for reasons detrimental to his reputation in violation of constitutional due process. The policeman claimed that derogatory information placed in his employment file had led to his discharge from another police department and subsequently blocked other employment opportunities. He neither alleged nor proved, however, that the derogatory information was false. The district court rendered judgment against the policeman, but the court of appeals reversed.

Question: Does due process require a hearing for a nontenured public employee who is discharged for reasons that stigmatize his reputation but are indisputably accurate?

Decision: No. Per curiam opinion. Vote: 5–4, Brennan, Marshall, Stewart, and Stevens dissenting.

Reasons: The due process clause entitles a public employee whose reputation is stigmatized in connection with his dismissal to a hearing for the purpose of refuting the derogatory charges and thus clearing his name: "If the hearing mandated by the Due Process Clause is to serve any useful purpose, there must be some factual dispute between an employer and a discharged employee that has some significant bearing on the employee's reputation." In this case, the policeman failed to challenge the substantial truth of the derogatory material in question. Since the policeman could not in any event have cleared his name, therefore, no constitutionally cognizable injury was suffered as a result of the denial of a hearing.

Elections and Voting Rights

The landmark 1962 decision of the Supreme Court in *Baker* v. *Carr*[45] established the justiciability of challenges to the apportionment of legislative bodies under the equal protection clause. In subsequent decisions, the Court held that a one-person, one-vote rule is constitutionally commanded in the apportionment of legislative bodies exercising general government powers.[46] Political gerrymandering— apportionment plans drawn to create "safe" Democratic and Repub-

---

[45] 369 U.S. 186.
[46] See Hadley v. Junior College District, 397 U.S. 50 (1970); Reynolds v. Sims, 377 U.S. 533 (1964); Wesberry v. Sanders, 376 U.S. 1 (1964).

lican seats in proportion to the statewide strengths of the two parties —is a related phenomenon the Court has confronted and generally approved.[47] In three decisions this term, the Court addressed offshoots of these basic principles.

Racial gerrymandering was attacked as a type of reverse discrimination in *United Jewish Organizations of Williamsburgh, Inc.* v. *Carey*, 430 U.S. 144 (1977). In an effort to remedy past racial discrimination, New York enacted a reapportionment plan drawn along racial lines to ensure the election of black candidates in rough proportion to their percentage of the electoral population. Hasidic Jews, whose electoral strength was diluted by the plan, claimed that the constitutional prohibition against racial discrimination barred gerrymandering for the purpose of ensuring a racial group a quota of electoral victories. Rejecting that claim, the Court concluded, in a plurality opinion by Justice White, that racially gerrymandered reapportionment plans that do not unfairly dilute the voting strength of any racial group as a whole pass constitutional scrutiny. Racial gerrymandering is permissible, the plurality asserted, whether or not it is designed to remedy past discrimination.

It will be regrettable if the plurality view becomes that of the Court. Racial gerrymandering encourages political division along racial lines, among both citizens and legislators. Such gerrymandering mocks efforts to promote racial harmony and sustains irrational racial considerations that infect the electoral process.

Frustrated by their failure to obtain a charter for the county of Niagara, city dwellers sought victory through an extension of the one-person, one-vote principle to referendum elections. New York State requires concurrent majorities of both city and noncity dwellers to adopt a county charter by referendum. The more numerous city dwellers of Niagara claimed that the dual majority rule gave proportionately more weight to noncity voters in contravention of the equal protection principle of one-person, one-vote. In *Lockport* v. *Citizens for Community Action*, 430 U.S. 259 (1977), a unanimous Court asserted that one-person, one-vote principles apply to the election of representatives but have little relevance in elections in which voters directly express their will.

Some of the recent decisions of the Court evince a desire to extricate the federal judiciary from the political thicket of reapportionment.[48] The decision this term in *Connor* v. *Finch*, 431 U.S. 407

---

[47] Gaffney v. Cummings, 412 U.S. 735 (1973).

[48] See Mahan v. Howell, 410 U.S. 315 (1973); White v. Regester, 412 U.S. 755 (1973); Whitcomb v. Chavis, 403 U.S. 124 (1971).

(1977), advanced that goal. There the Court invalidated a judicially fashioned reapportionment plan on account of its failure to adhere to a rule of strict population equality among electoral districts. The reaffirmation by the Court of the principle that legislatively devised plans are permitted deviations from population equality unavailable to federal courts invited state legislatures to adopt their own reapportionment plans.

United Jewish Organizations of Williamsburgh, Inc. v. Carey, 430 U.S. 144 (1977)

Facts: Section 5 of the Voting Rights Act prohibits certain states or political subdivisions from implementing a legislative reapportionment plan absent a finding by a federal district court or the U.S. attorney general that it has neither a racially discriminatory purpose nor effect. In seeking to comply with section 5, New York State adopted a reapportionment plan for congressional, state senate, and state assembly seats. As applicable to Kings County, the plan was purposely drawn on racial lines to include several districts with substantial nonwhite majorities of approximately 75 percent. Since the county had exhibited a history of voting by racial blocs, the state used racial classifications in drawing district lines to assure nonwhites the opportunity to elect members of their groups in numbers reasonably proportionate to the percentage of nonwhites in the county.

The Kings County reapportionment plan caused a substantial reduction in the number of Hasidic Jews formerly located in just one district. They brought suit in federal district court, claiming that the plan was unconstitutional because it diluted their voting power solely for the purpose of achieving a racial quota and because the electoral districts were drawn solely on the basis of race. The district court dismissed the complaint. The court of appeals affirmed, noting that the challenged plan left approximately 70 percent of the senate and assembly districts in Kings County with white majorities, although whites represented only 65 percent of the population of the county.

Question: Was New York's legislative reapportionment plan, as applicable to Kings County, unconstitutional?

Decision: No. Plurality opinion by Justice White. Vote: 7–1, Brennan, Blackmun, Stewart, Powell, and Rehnquist concurring, Burger dissenting. Marshall did not participate.

Reasons: The Voting Rights Act was designed by Congress to remedy a long history of racial discrimination in voting. In reviewing reapportionment plans under section 5, the Court implicitly accepted the proposition in *City of Richmond* v. *United States,* 422 U.S. 358 (1975), and *Beer* v. *United States,* 425 U.S. 130 (1976), that racial criteria may constitutionally be used to establish districts that fairly reflect the voting strength of the black community, whether or not necessary to remedy past unconstitutional apportionments.

In addition, the statewide reapportionment plan passed constitutional muster without regard to section 5 of the Voting Rights Act. The plan did not stigmatize whites or any other race and worked no discrimination in voting violative of either the Fourteenth or Fifteenth amendments. Although the plan was purposely drawn to enhance the electoral prospects of nonwhite candidates in certain districts in Kings County, it did not minimize or unfairly dilute white voting strength as a whole, either in Kings County or in the state. In districts with a nonwhite majority, given voting by racial blocs, the plan reduced the likelihood that white voters could elect a member of their own race. "But as long as whites in Kings County, as a group, were provided with fair representation, we cannot conclude that there was a cognizable discrimination against whites or an abridgement of their right to vote on grounds of race."

While supporting or opposing a candidate on account of race may be regrettable, states are not constitutionally prohibited from seeking to alleviate the consequences of such voting behavior through districting plans designed to achieve a fair allocation of political power between white and nonwhite voters.

Lockport v. Citizens for Community Action, 430 U.S. 259 (1977)

Facts: The allocation of government power in New York counties is generally divided between a county legislature and the constituent cities, villages, and towns of the county. Any new county charter that would change this allocation must be approved in a referendum election by separate majorities of the county voters who live within and without the cities.

A proposed charter for the county of Niagara was defeated for failure to win a majority of noncity voters. Niagara city dwellers successfully attacked the concurrent majority requirement in federal district court on the ground that it violated the one-person, one-vote mandate of the equal protection clause.

Question: Does the New York concurrent majority requirement for approval of new county charters violate the equal protection clause?

Decision: No. Opinion by Justice Stewart. Vote: 9–0.

Reasons: In *Reynolds* v. *Sims*, 377 U.S. 533 (1964), and subsequent cases, the Court established the general principle that in legislative elections the equal protection clause requires that all votes be accorded substantially equal weight. This one-person, one-vote principle, however,

> applicable in gauging the fairness of an election involving the choice of legislative representatives is of limited relevance . . . in analyzing the propriety of recognizing distinctive voter interests in a "single-shot" referendum. In a referendum, the expression of voter will is direct, and there is no need to assure that the voters' views will be adequately represented through their representatives in the legislature.

In *Salyer Land Co.* v. *Tulare Lake Basin Water Storage District*, 410 U.S. 719 (1973), the Court recognized the fact that in elections having a disproportionate impact on an identifiable group of voters, regulations of the franchise pass equal protection scrutiny unless they work an invidious discrimination against particular voters. The effect on city voters of the adoption or rejection of a county charter in New York will generally be different from the effect on noncity voters. The cities have substantial autonomy and often perform functions within their jurisdiction that the county may perform for noncity residents. Historically, towns and villages have provided major social services, and provisions of proposed new charters frequently transfer these duties to the county government. The reorganization of county government thus may make the provider of public services in towns and villages more remote and less subject to the influence of voters there. The challenged concurrent majority provisions simply recognize the realities of the substantially differing electoral interests of city and noncity voters. "Granting to these provisions the presumption of constitutionality to which every duly enacted state and federal law is entitled, we are unable to conclude that they violate the Equal Protection Clause of the Fourteenth Amendment."

Connor v. Finch, 431 U.S. 407 (1977)

Facts: In 1965, a federal district court held that under *Reynolds v. Sims,* 377 U.S. 533 (1964), a Mississippi state legislative apportionment statute violated the one-person, one-vote mandate of the equal protection clause. After the failure of the state legislature to enact a constitutionally acceptable reapportionment plan and additional protracted litigation, the district court adopted a permanent plan for the state senate and house of representatives, providing for a maximum deviation from population equality in senatorial and house districts of 16.5 percent and 19.3 percent, respectively. The district court concluded that these disparities were justified by the interest of the state in maintaining the inviolability of county lines. Plaintiffs sought review of the court-ordered reapportionment plan on the ground, *inter alia,* that it failed to implement the one-person, one-vote standards of *Reynolds v. Sims.*

Question: Did the questioned reapportionment plan represent a proper exercise of equitable discretion by the district court in formulating a decree to remedy an abridgement of the one-person, one-vote mandate of the equal protection clause?

Decision: No. Opinion by Justice Stewart. Vote: 7–1, Powell dissenting. Rehnquist did not participate.

Reasons: In *Chapman v. Meir,* 420 U.S. 1 (1975), the Court held that court-ordered reapportionment plans must satisfy stricter standards of population equality than those applicable to legislatively devised plans. While statutory reapportionment plans for state legislatures may, without justification, have population deviations among districts of up to 10 percent, court-ordered plans can deviate from approximate population equality only to the minimum extent necessary to advance historically significant state policy or to accommodate unique features.

In *Mahan v. Howell,* 410 U.S. 315 (1973), the Court sustained a statutory reapportionment plan for the house of delegates that had a population deviation of 16.5 percent among districts. There was uncontradicted evidence that the deviation was the minimum necessary to achieve the legitimate state goal of maintaining political subdivisions that exercised responsibilities incident to the operation of state government. Here, in contrast, the district court rejected a plan offered by plaintiffs that had greater population equality and less county fragmentation than its own plan.

In the absence of a convincing justification for its continued adherence to a plan that even in state policy terms is less efficacious than another plan actually proposed, there can be no alternative but to set aside the District Court's decree for its failure to embody the equitable discretion necessary to effectuate the established standards of the Equal Protection Clause.

Racial Discrimination

The major decisions of the Court concerning racial discrimination this term were carefully dissected for hints as to the attitude of the Court toward so-called reverse discrimination. Review has been granted in the widely publicized case of *Regents, University of California* v. *Bakke*,[49] in which the constitutionality of quotas favoring disadvantaged minorities in admissions to a state medical school is at issue. In upholding the use of racial gerrymandering, a plurality of the Court gave constitutional endorsement to reverse discrimination in *United Jewish Organizations of Williamsburgh, Inc.* v. *Carey*, 430 U.S. 144 (1977), without a finding of prior unconstitutional conduct. But the decision in *Casteneda* v. *Partida*, 430 U.S. 482 (1977), conveyed a different message. There the Court embraced the use of statistics to establish a prima facie case of unconstitutional discrimination against Mexican-Americans in the selection of grand jurors. In rejecting a defense built upon the prevalence of Mexican-American officials responsible for selection of grand juries, however, the Court disavowed any constitutional presumption that individuals of one definable group will not discriminate against other members of the same group. This conclusion undermines the claim that white citizens lack constitutional protection against reverse discrimination simply because they generally occupy a majority of elective and appointive offices.

Last term, in *Washington* v. *Davis*, 426 U.S. 229 (1976), the Court held that an equal protection claim is not established by proof that government action has a racially disproportionate effect; proof of a racially discriminatory purpose or intent is required. This term, in *Arlington Heights* v. *Metropolitan Housing Development Corp.*, 429 U.S. 252 (1977), the Court embraced the use of a wide range of evidence to infer a tainted purpose or intent: historical background, the sequence of events preceding the contested action, and its legislative or administrative history. Many states and municipalities,

---

[49] No. 76-811, 45 U.S.L.W. 3570 (February 22, 1977).

however, fail to maintain official legislative or administrative histories. The Court noted that in "extraordinary instances" plaintiffs might be allowed to compel testimony from legislative or administrative officials to explain the purpose of official action alleged to be racially tainted.

School desegregation remedies were given a mixed reception by the Court. The decision in *Milliken* v. *Bradley*, 433 U.S. 267 (1977), endorsed a broad desegregation remedy that required the adoption of remedial education programs, in-service teacher training, a system of testing free of racial or cultural bias, and counseling and career guidance for students. In *Dayton Board of Education* v. *Brinkman*, 433 U.S. 406 (1977), however, the Court held that desegregation orders altering pupil assignments should seek only the racial mix that would have existed absent the constitutional violation.

The quest by minority groups and women to hurdle seniority barriers in seeking access to jobs and obtaining promotions[50] was partially stymied as the Court interpreted the 1964 Civil Rights Act in *International Brotherhood of Teamsters* v. *United States*, 431 U.S. 324 (1977). Although Title VII of the act generally prohibits employment discrimination on the basis of race or sex, it offers an immunity to bona fide seniority systems. This immunity, the Court concluded, shields these seniority systems from attack under Title VII, even if they perpetuate the effects of past discrimination. The Court added, however, that a seniority system forfeits this protection if it is infected with a racially discriminatory intent at its genesis or in its maintenance.[51]

Casteneda v. *Partida*, 430 U.S. 482 (1977)

Facts: Indicted by a grand jury in Hildago County, Texas, and convicted of burglary, Partida (a Mexican-American) sought a new trial on the ground that the grand jury selection process unconstitutionally discriminated against Mexican-Americans. Statistics adduced as evidence showed that 79.1 percent of the population of Hildago County was Mexican-American; that during the eleven years preceding the indictment of Partida only 39 percent of those chosen

---

[50] See *Washington Post*, July 10, 1977.

[51] In an interpretive memorandum, the Equal Employment Opportunity Commission has embraced a broad view of the types of evidence sufficient to trigger an inference of discriminatory intent in the genesis or maintenance of a seniority system. See 46 U.S.L.W. 2028 (July 19, 1977).

for grand jury service in the county were Mexican-Americans; that 50 percent of the grand jurors who indicted Partida were Mexican-Americans; and that Mexican-Americans were generally poor, possessed undesirable jobs, lived in substandard housing, and attained low levels of education. A Texas state court held that these statistics failed to establish a prima facie case of unconstitutional discrimination. It noted that Mexican-Americans held many elective positions in Hildago County, three of the five jury commissioners who selected the grand jury that indicted Partida were Mexican-Americans, and a majority of the petit jury and the judge who tried Partida were Mexican-Americans. The state court refused to presume that Mexican-Americans would discriminate against their own kind.

In a federal habeas corpus suit, a federal court of appeals upheld Partida's claim of unconstitutional discrimination against Mexican-Americans. The court noted that under the Texas system of grand jury selection, jury commissioners possess wide discretion in choosing grand jurors on the basis of moral character, literacy, and other subjective factors. The court of appeals reasoned that this fact, combined with the statistics showing a disproportionately low percentage of Mexican-Americans on Hildago County grand juries, established a prima facie case of unconstitutional discrimination that the state failed to rebut. It rejected the argument that the prima facie case could be rebutted simply because Mexican-Americans constituted a governing majority in Hildago County.

Question: Did the statistical and other evidence in this case justify the inference that Texas unconstitutionally discriminated against Mexican-Americans in the selection of grand jurors in Hildago County?

Decision: Yes. Opinion by Justice Blackmun. Vote: 5–4, Burger, Stewart, Powell, and Rehnquist dissenting.

Reasons: Official action is not unconstitutional solely because it has a racially disproportionate impact. A purpose or intent to discriminate on account of race must be proven to establish a violation of the equal protection clause. A racially discriminatory purpose or intent may, however, be established by statistics unexplainable by other theories. In the context of grand jury selection, the Court has held that a prima facie case of unconstitutional discrimination is established if the defendant shows that the "procedure used resulted in substantial under-representation of the race or of the identifiable group to which he belongs." This requires proof that the group constitutes a distinct class singled out for different treatment under the laws and a comparison of the "proportion of the group in the total population to the proportion called to serve as grand jurors, over a significant period of time." A selection procedure that is susceptible to abuse supports a presumption of discrimination raised by statistical evidence: "Once the defendant has shown substantial underrepresentation of his group, he has made out a prima facie case of discriminatory purpose, and the burden then shifts to the State to rebut that case."

The application of these principles to this case justifies a finding of unconstitutional discrimination in the selection of grand jurors. Mexican-Americans are a clearly identifiable class who suffer from economic and other disadvantages. The subjective process of grand jury selection provided an easy opportunity to discriminate against Mexican-Americans. The underrepresentation of that class on grand juries in Hildago County during an eleven-year period was substantial: 79.1 percent Mexican-Americans in the county population compared with 39 percent of those summoned for grand jury service. The probability that this disparity was to be explained by chance is less than 10 percent. These facts established a prima facie case of purposeful discrimination that the state failed to rebut. It failed to obtain testimony from the grand jury commissioners or other evidence that might explain the underrepresentation of Mexican-Americans on racially neutral grounds, such as a lack of literacy or prior criminal records. The mere fact that Mexican-Americans constituted a governing majority in Hildago County did not fill this gap in the evidence. It cannot be presumed as a matter of law that individuals of one definable group will not discriminate against other group members. Moreover, the record failed to establish the period in which Mexican-Americans enjoyed governing-majority status in the county or the power of the offices they held. "Under the facts presented in this case, the 'governing majority' theory is not developed fully enough to satisfy the State's burden of rebuttal."

Arlington Heights v. *Metropolitan Housing Development Corporation*, 429 U.S. 252 (1977)

Facts: The Village of Arlington Heights, a predominantly white suburb of Chicago, denied a developer's request to rezone a fifteen-acre parcel from single-family to multiple-family classification to allow him to build low- and moderate-income housing. The developer, a prospective black tenant, and others brought suit against the village, claiming that its denial was racially discriminatory, in violation of the equal protection clause of the Fourteenth Amendment. After trial, the district court rejected the claims of the plaintiffs, finding that the zoning denial was prompted by a desire to protect property values and the integrity of the zoning plan of the village. The court of appeals reversed, observing that the denial had a racially discriminatory effect, because a disproportionate percentage of black families in the area would qualify as eligible tenants in the proposed housing development. It held that once a racially discriminatory effect was shown, the denial could be constitutionally sustained only if advancement of a compelling state interest required it. Protection of property values and maintaining a zoning plan, the court of appeals concluded, were not compelling interests.

Questions: (1) Did any plaintiff have standing to maintain the suit? (2) Did the court of appeals err in holding that government action having a racially discriminatory effect, without more, may violate the equal protection clause?

Decision: Yes to both questions. Opinion by Justice Powell. Vote: 7–1, White dissenting. Stevens did not participate.

Reasons: A challenge to standing was not raised in the court of appeals. Questions of standing, however, express a concern over limiting the jurisdiction of federal courts to "cases" or "controversies." Thus, standing may be challenged and considered initially in the Supreme Court.

To obtain standing, a plaintiff must allege injury caused by the challenged action of the defendant that is "fairly traceable to the defendant's acts or omissions." The prospective black tenant satisfied this test. He alleged and testified that he would probably move to the planned low- and moderate-income housing development that was thwarted by the village's rezoning denial. The lack of a new housing opportunity constituted injury which was fairly traceable to the contested zoning decision because of a "substantial probability" that the proposed housing development would have otherwise been built.

With regard to the merits, *Washington v. Davis*, 426 U.S. 229 (1976), established that government action does not violate the equal protection clause solely because it has a racially disproportionate effect. "Proof of racially discriminatory intent or purpose is required to show a violation of the Equal Protection Clause." Evidence relevant to this issue, of course, would include the historical background of the action, the specific sequence of events preceding the challenged decision, and its legislative or administrative history.

In this case, for example, if the rezoning denial reflected a clear and unexplained departure from earlier zoning decisions, or if the parcel at issue had been downgraded to single-family homes shortly after the developer's plans were publicized, a racially discriminatory purpose might properly have been inferred. But where, as here, such evidence is lacking, the racially discriminatory effect of a rezoning denial is without constitutional significance.

The Court also concluded that if an official decision is partially infected with a racially discriminatory purpose, it should nonetheless be constitutionally sustained if the defendants can establish that the absence of an impermissible purpose would not have altered that decision.

Milliken v. Bradley, 433 U.S. 267 (1977)

Facts: A federal district court found that both the Detroit school board and the state of Michigan had taken unconstitutional actions intended to effect racial segregation in the Detroit public schools. As part of its remedy for desegregation, the district court ordered the board to adopt four compensatory education programs: a remedial reading program to eradicate the effects of past discrimination; an in-service training program for teachers and administrators to ensure identical treatment of all students in desegregated schools; a revised system of testing that was free from racial or cultural bias; and a counseling and career-guidance program to deal with psychological stress and to provide information about new vocational and technical programs available under the desegregation plan. The court ordered that the cost of these four programs be shared equally by the board of education and the state. In the court of appeals, the state argued unsuccessfully that the desegregation order of the district court exceeded its equitable powers and violated the Eleventh Amendment in requiring partial state funding of the remedial programs.

Question: Were the desegregation orders of the district court regarding compensatory education programs both within its equitable discretion and consistent with the Eleventh Amendment?

Decision: Yes. Opinion by Chief Justice Burger. Vote: 9–0.

Reasons: Federal courts possess broad power to formulate equitable remedies to eradicate the effects of unconstitutional racial discrimination. The nature of the remedy depends upon the scope of the constitutional violation and must be limited to restoring the victims

91

of discriminatory conduct to the positions they would have occupied absent the violation.

Here the questioned remedial education programs were all designed to overcome the effects of past unconstitutional school segregation. Racially segregated educational facilities are inherently unequal: "Children who have been . . . educationally and culturally set apart from the larger community will inevitably acquire habits of speech, conduct, and attitudes reflecting their cultural isolation." The reading, in-service training, testing, and career-counseling programs were appropriate tools for eliminating the deleterious educational consequences of unconstitutional segregation in Detroit schools.

The Eleventh Amendment claim stems from the order requiring the state to fund 50 percent of the compensatory education programs. That amendment generally prohibits federal courts from entertaining damage suits against a state based on past conduct, but it raises no barrier to federal court orders that operate prospectively and serve to eliminate the effects of unconstitutional action by the state. Although such prospective relief may require expenditures from the state treasury, the Eleventh Amendment may not be invoked to prevent this result.

In a related decision, *Dayton Board of Education* v. *Brinkman*, 433 U.S. 406 (1977), the Court established a general standard for determining the appropriate distribution of students by race in school systems subject to desegregation orders, holding that the racial distribution should reflect the situation that would have existed absent the constitutional violation committed by state or local school authorities.

International Brotherhood of Teamsters v. *United States*, 431 U.S. 324 (1977)

Facts: The United States brought suit against a motor freight company and the Teamsters Union, both of whom were alleged to be engaging in a pattern and practice of employment discrimination against blacks and Spanish-surnamed Americans, in violation of Title VII of the 1964 Civil Rights Act. The company was charged with discriminating against the minority groups in the hiring of long-haul drivers. Members of minority groups who obtained jobs were alleged to be restricted to lower-paying, less desirable positions, such as those of servicemen or local drivers. In addition, the seniority system established by the collective-bargaining agreement between the company and the union was attacked because it impeded the transfer of members of minority groups to more desirable long-haul jobs. The district court found that the hiring practices and seniority system of the company violated Title VII. The seniority system, the court reasoned, perpetuated the effects of discrimination in the hiring of long-haul employees that occurred before enactment of Title VII, thus "locking" minority workers into inferior jobs and creating enormous disincentives for transfer. For purposes of determining the order of layoffs, recalls, and bidding on particular jobs, the system made seniority within a bargaining unit controlling. As a result, a local driver or serviceman who transferred to a long-haul job would forfeit all his bargaining unit seniority and start at the bottom of the long-haul seniority list. The court of appeals affirmed and ordered extensive remedial relief.

Questions: (1) Did the company engage in a pattern and practice of discrimination in the employment of long-haul drivers in violation of Title VII? (2) Did the questioned seniority system as applied to those who had been discriminated against before passage of the act unlawfully perpetuate the effects of past discrimination?

Decision: Yes to the first question and no to the second. Opinion by Justice Stewart. Vote: 7–2, Marshall and Brennan dissenting in part.

Reasons: Section 703(a) of Title VII makes unlawful discrimination by an employer against an individual on the basis of race or national origin. The United States is authorized under section 707 to bring suit challenging a "pattern or practice" of employment discrimination; to prove a pattern or practice, the government must establish that racial discrimination is a "company's standard operating procedure—the regular rather than the unusual practice." Here the government alleged that a motor freight company systematically discriminated against members of minority groups in hiring, promotion, and transfer, especially with regard to long-haul jobs. Its evidence showed that virtually all long-haul drivers were white, while the company's workforce was 5 percent black and 4 percent Spanish-surnamed. Whereas only 39 percent of nonminority employees held disfavored jobs within the city and as servicemen, 83 percent of the black employees and 78 percent of the Spanish-surnamed held such jobs. These statistics, coupled with proof of forty specific instances of discrimination, justified the inference that the company had engaged in a pattern and practice of discrimination in its hiring and promotion policies. Any black or Spanish-surnamed employee injured by this discrimination may receive back pay and retroactive seniority under the authority of *Franks* v. *Bowman Transportation Co.*, 424 U.S. 747 (1976).

The seniority system is claimed to violate Title VII insofar as it perpetuates the effects of employment discrimination that occurred before its enactment. The system allocates the best jobs, greatest protection against layoffs, and other advantages to employees with the longest service as long-haul drivers. Virtually all of these employees are white because of discrimination against minorities before passage of the act. The questioned seniority system thus has a racially discriminatory effect that would ordinarily violate Title VII as construed in *Griggs* v. *Duke Power Co.*, 401 U.S. 424 (1971). Section 703(h) confers on seniority systems a limited immunity from attack under Title VII, however, by providing that the operation of a bona fide seniority system, adopted without an intention to discriminate on the basis of race or national origin, shall be lawful despite any discriminatory effects. The legislative history of Title VII makes clear that an otherwise neutral, legitimate seniority system does not lose its section 703(h) protection simply because it perpetuates discrimination that occurred before the act was passed.

> It is conceded that the seniority system did not have its genesis in racial discrimination, and that it was negotiated and has been maintained free from any illegal purpose. In these circumstances, the single fact that the system extends no retroactive seniority to pre-Act discriminatees does not make it unlawful.

On remand, the district court must formulate a new remedial decree. The government's proof of the pattern and practice supports an inference that all the employment decisions made by the company when its discriminatory policy was in effect were unlawful. Thus, any employee alleged to have been discriminated against during this period who was denied a long-haul position or other employment is entitled to relief, including retroactive seniority, absent proof by the company that its decision was based on lawful reasons. A nonapplicant for employment or transfer, moreover, may also obtain an award of retroactive seniority. He must show that he was a potential victim of unlawful discrimination and would have applied for a job or transfer absent discriminatory policies of the employer. When that burden is met, retroactive seniority may be awarded unless the employer proves that the nonapplicant would have been denied employment or transfer for legitimate reasons.

Sex Discrimination

Three notable developments marked the treatment of sex discrimination by the Court during the 1976–1977 term. In *Craig v. Boren,* 429 U.S. 160 (1976), the Court specifically held for the first time that males are entitled to the same constitutional protection against sex discrimination as females, at least when so-called benign discrimination is not at issue. This holding is somewhat anomalous, since males, unlike females, dominate elective office and are generally perceived not to be threatened by the majoritarian political process.[52] In other cases, the Court has endorsed special equal protection status only for groups that are politically weak or that have been subject to a history of unequal treatment.[53] In the wake of *Craig,* men are likely to invoke their elevated constitutional status in divorce cases, in which women have traditionally been favored in the award of alimony and the custody of children and in the disposition of property.[54]

A second development of note was the pronouncement of a clear standard for the evaluation of claims of sex discrimination under the equal protection clause of the Fourteenth Amendment. Since its 1971 decision in *Reed v. Reed,*[55] the Court has required the government to justify classifications based on sex by more than mere rationality but less than a compelling state interest[56] to pass constitutional scrutiny.[57] In *Craig v. Boren,* the Court announced that classifications based on sex survive scrutiny under the equal protection clause only if they are substantially related to the achievement of important governmental objectives.

---

[52] In 1974, women were elected to 18 congressional seats, 1 governor's chair, and 596 seats in state legislatures. See U.S. Bureau of the Census, *A Statistical Portrait of Women in the U.S.,* 1976, p. 56.

[53] Minority racial groups (Casteneda v. Partida, 430 U.S. 482 [1977]; Hunter v. Erickson, 393 U.S. 385 [1969]), aliens (Graham v. Richardson, 403 U.S. 365 [1971]), and illegitimates (Trimble v. Gordon, 430 U.S. 762 [1977]) have been afforded heightened constitutional protection for this reason.

[54] In recent years, many fathers have organized to fight for equal rights in divorce. See *Washington Post,* December 14, 1975. A federal district court has held unconstitutional a provision of the Federal Bankruptcy Act that denies husbands but not wives the opportunity to discharge alimony debts (In re Wasserman, 46 U.S.L.W. 2073, August 23, 1977 [D.R.I. 1977]).

[55] 404 U.S. 71 (1971).

[56] A compelling state interest is demanded for suspect classifications, such as race or alienage, at least if benign discrimination is not involved. See note 53, above.

[57] See Frontiero v. Richardson, 411 U.S. 677 (1973); Stanton v. Stanton, 421 U.S. 7 (1975); Weinberger v. Wiesenfeld, 420 U.S. 636 (1975).

In a third development carrying implications for the adoption of the Equal Rights Amendment, the Court held unanimously, in *Califano* v. *Webster*, 430 U.S. 313 (1977), that benign sex discrimination that prefers women over men to ameliorate historical economic discrimination is constitutionally permissible.[58] Interestingly, it is open to question whether women could be preferred as a class under the Equal Rights Amendment,[59] which must be ratified by thirty-eight states before March 1979 to become effective.[60]

In two other cases that plowed established constitutional terrain, the Court held (1) in *Mathews* v. *De Castro*, 429 U.S. 181 (1977), that married women could be preferred over divorcees in the awarding of wife's insurance benefits under the Social Security Act, and (2) in *Califano* v. *Goldfarb*, 430 U.S. 199 (1977), that administrative convenience could not constitutionally excuse preferring widows to widowers in the payment of survivors' benefits under the same act.

Women fared poorly in statutory battles over sex discrimination. In *General Electric* v. *Gilbert*, 429 U.S. 125 (1976), the Court upheld an employer's prerogative to exclude disabilities arising from pregnancies from an employee disability insurance plan, a decision roundly condemned by feminist groups. Female employees had claimed that the exclusion violated Title VII of the 1964 Civil Rights Act.[61] In *Dothard* v. *Rawlinson*, 433 U.S. 321 (1977), another Title VII case, the Court struck down a requirement of a minimum height and weight for employment as a prison guard, but sustained a blanket exclusion of females from contact positions in the violent all-male security prisons of Alabama.

Craig v. *Boren*, 429 U.S. 160 (1976)

Facts: A licensed vendor of intoxicating beverages brought suit challenging the constitutionality of an Oklahoma statute that prohibited the sale of 3.2 percent beer to males under the age of twenty-

---

[58] At present, women earn substantially less than do men of comparable age, experience, and education working in the same occupation. See *A Statistical Portrait of Women*, pp. 45–46.

[59] The proposed amendment states: "Equality of Rights under the law shall not be denied or abridged by the United States or by any State on account of sex."

[60] As of this writing, the Equal Rights Amendment has been approved by thirty-five states. A few states have rescinded their approval. Whether the rescissions are effective is a political question solely for Congress to decide. See Coleman v. Miller, 307 U.S. 433 (1939).

[61] By a vote of 75–11, the Senate approved a bill on September 16, 1977, that would, in effect, overturn the *Gilbert* decision. See S. 995, 95th Congress, 1st session (1977).

one and to females under the age of eighteen. Seeking declaratory and injunctive relief, the vendor claimed that the statutory age differential discriminated against males in violation of the equal protection clause of the Fourteenth Amendment. In upholding the statute, the district court found that it substantially promoted traffic safety because males between the ages of eighteen and twenty-one were more likely than their female counterparts to drive while intoxicated.

Question: Does the challenged Oklahoma statute unconstitutionally discriminate against males in violation of the equal protection clause?

Decision: Yes. Opinion by Justice Brennan. Vote: 7–2, Burger and Rehnquist dissenting.

Reasons: The Court first addressed the issue of whether the vendor had standing to attack the statute by asserting the constitutional rights of third parties, namely, males between the ages of eighteen and twenty-one. Limitations on the assertion by a litigant of the rights of third parties are not "constitutionally mandated, but rather stem from a salutary 'rule of self-restraint' designed to minimize unwarranted intervention into controversies where applicable constitutional questions are ill-defined and speculative." These prudential considerations are inapplicable here because the constitutional issue has been sharply defined by the district court, where the standing of the vendor was not challenged. Additionally, the vendor falls into a narrow category of litigants entitled to attack a statute by advancing the constitutional rights of third parties. The statute causes him economic injury by restricting the market for the sale of beer. Under *Warth* v. *Seldin*, 422 U.S. 490 (1975), and *Griswold* v. *Connecticut*, 381 U.S. 479 (1965), the vendor may thus assert the concomitant interests of third parties that would be adversely affected should the constitutional attack fail. Here those interests are the rights of males eighteen to twenty-one years old to be free from sex discrimination in the purchase of 3.2 percent beer.

Under *Reed* v. *Reed*, 404 U.S. 71 (1971), the challenged statutory discrimination against males survives equal protection scrutiny only if it is "substantially related" to the achievement of "important governmental objectives." Although enhancement of traffic safety is an important governmental objective, prohibiting the purchase of 3.2 percent beer by males but not females between the ages of eighteen and twenty-one has, at best, a tenuous relationship to this goal. Statistical evidence introduced at trial establishes that 0.18

percent of females and 2 percent of males in this age group are arrested for alcohol-related driving offenses. While this disparity is not trivial, it fails to justify using maleness as a classification in regulating the sale of alcohol. Traffic safety is not substantially advanced by denying the right to purchase 3.2 percent beer to all males simply because 2 percent may create a traffic danger. Thus, under *Reed*, the challenged statute violates the equal protection rights of these young males.

The Twenty-first Amendment does not alter this conclusion. Generally speaking, it forbids the transportation of intoxicating liquors into a state for delivery or use there in violation of state law. It authorizes states to regulate alcoholic beverages to an extent not otherwise permitted by the commerce clause (*Hostetter* v. *Idlewild Bon Voyage Liquor Corp.*, 377 U.S. 324 [1964]), and strengthens their authority to prohibit certain sexual performances from occurring where liquor is dispensed (*California* v. *LaRue*, 409 U.S. 109 [1972]). It does not reduce the safeguards against discrimination on account of race or sex secured by the equal protection clause, however.

Califano v. *Webster*, 430 U.S. 313 (1977)

Facts: Under section 215 of the Social Security Act, certain female wage earners receive more generous old-age insurance benefits than similarly situated male wage earners. A federal district court held that the more generous benefit formula for females was irrational and in violation of the due process clause of the Fifth Amendment.

Question: Does section 215 unconstitutionally discriminate against male wage earners?

Decision: No. Per curiam opinion. Vote: 9–0.

Reasons: The due process clause requires that sex-based classifications serve "important governmental objectives and . . . be substantially related to the achievement of these objectives." In *Kahn* v. *Shevin*, 416 U.S. 351 (1974), the Court recognized that reducing the financial disparity between men and women caused by historical economic discrimination against the latter qualifies as an important government objective. Section 215 was designed to compensate women for historical economic discrimination that channeled them into low-paying jobs. It thus passes constitutional scrutiny under the due process clause.

Mathews v. *De Castro*, 429 U.S. 181 (1976)

Facts: Under section 202(b)(1) of the Social Security Act, a married woman caring for a dependent child is entitled to a wife's insurance benefits if her husband qualifies for old-age or disability benefits. A divorced wife in the same circumstances, however, is denied a wife's insurance benefits unless she has attained the age of sixty-two. That discrimination against divorced women was successfully attacked in federal district court on the ground that it violated the due process clause of the Fifth Amendment.

Question: Does section 202(b)(1) invidiously discriminate against divorced wives in violation of constitutional due process?

Decision: No. Opinion by Justice Stewart. Vote: 9–0.

Reasons: Congress has broad latitude in devising spending programs to advance the general welfare. It may treat classes of persons differently so long as the differences have a rational basis. The primary objective of social security old-age and disability insurance benefits is the protection of workers and their families from economic hardship created by loss of earnings. Section 202(b)(1) is consistent with this objective. The married wife's benefits are triggered when she must meet additional economic burdens caused by her husband's retirement or disability:

> Congress could rationally have decided that the resultant loss of family income, the extra expense that often attends illness and old age, and the consequent disruption in the family's economic well being that may occur when the husband stops working justify monthly payments to a wife who together with her husband must still care for a dependent child.

A divorced wife, in contrast to a married one, generally faces no economic burden or disruption associated with her husband's retirement or disability because they typically live separate lives. Although in particular circumstances a husband's old-age or disability may cause his divorced wife economic hardships, Congress "could rationally decide that [their] problems remained less pressing than those faced by women who continue to live with their husbands." In addition, due process permits statutory classifications that facilitate objective and simple administration of a public welfare program, despite their exclusion of some whose factual circumstances are indistinguishable from those of eligible recipients.

Califano v. *Goldfarb*, 430 U.S. 199 (1977)

Facts: Under the Social Security Act, 42 U.S. Code 401–431, survivors' benefits based on the earnings of a deceased husband are payable to his widow whether or not she was economically dependent on him. In contrast, survivors' benefits based on the earnings of a deceased wife are payable to the widower only if she was providing at least half of his support. A three-judge federal district court held that the act unconstitutionally discriminated against female wage earners by affording them less protection for their surviving spouses than is provided to male workers.

Question: Is the discrimination between male and female wage earners for purposes of paying survivors' benefits under the Social Security Act unconstitutional?

Decision: Yes. Plurality opinion by Justice Brennan. Vote: 5–4, Stevens concurring, Rehnquist, Burger, Stewart, and Blackmun dissenting.

Reasons: Frontiero v. *Richardson*, 411 U.S. 677 (1973), and *Weinberger* v. *Wiesenfeld*, 420 U.S. 636 (1975), condemned presumptions that men are more likely than women to be the primary supporters of their spouses and children for the purpose of serving administrative convenience in allocating benefits. Such presumptions rest on archaic notions of male and female roles in society and cause dissimilar treatment of men and women who are similarly situated. The contested provisions of the Social Security Act are indistinguishable from the statutes invalidated in *Frontiero* and *Wiesenfeld*. They operate to deprive women wage earners of protection for their families which similarly situated male wage earners are granted. The sex-based discrimination was intended solely to aid administrative convenience in seeking to limit survivors' benefits to spouses who were in fact economically dependent on a deceased wage earner; that purpose cannot justify sex discrimination under the due process clause of the Fifth Amendment.

The Court rejected the argument that the different treatment of male and female wage earners was benign sex discrimination designed to remedy the financial needs of nondependent widows, which are arguably greater than those of widowers.

General Electric Co. v. *Gilbert*, 429 U.S. 125 (1976)

Facts: The employee disability insurance plan of General Electric (GE) for nonoccupational sickness or accidents denies protection for disabilities arising from pregnancy. Female employees of GE brought suit claiming that the exclusion of pregnancy-related disabilities constituted sex discrimination in violation of Title VII, section 703(a)(1), of the Civil Rights Act of 1964. That section makes it unlawful for an employer "to discriminate against any individual with respect to his compensation, terms, conditions, or privileges of employment, because of such individual's . . . sex. . . ." Although finding that the cost of GE's disability insurance plan per female employee was at least as high, if not higher, than the cost per male employee, the district court upheld the claim of sex discrimination. The court of appeals affirmed.

Question: Does exclusion by General Electric of pregnancy-related disabilities from coverage under its employee disability insurance plan constitute sex discrimination in violation of section 703(a)(1)?

Decision: No. Opinion by Justice Rehnquist. Vote: 6–3, Brennan, Marshall, and Stevens dissenting.

Reasons: Although Congress failed to specify whether the concept of discrimination in section 703(a)(1) was broader than the constitutional concept of discrimination embraced by the equal protection clause of the Fourteenth Amendment, the constitutional concept is quite relevant to its interpretation. In *Geduldig* v. *Aiello*, 417 U.S. 484 (1974), the Court concluded that the failure of a state disability insurance system to include pregnancy-related disabilities in its coverage did not constitute sex discrimination within the meaning of the equal protection clause. This was because the exclusion did not divide the potential beneficiaries into groups based upon sex; rather, the division created two groups of potential beneficiaries based upon pregnancy—pregnant women and nonpregnant persons. This classification was not sex-based. Although the first group is exclusively female, the second includes members of both sexes. By the same reasoning, the failure of GE to include pregnancy-related disabilities in its disability insurance plan is not per se a sex-based discrimination.

Proof that a classification based on pregnancy is a mere pretext designed to effect a sex-based discrimination, however, would justify its condemnation under section 703(a)(1). The effects of a pregnancy-based classification may be evidence of an unlawful intent or invidious discrimination against female employees. In this case, however, such evidence is lacking. Even without the coverage of pregnancy-related disabilities, the insurance plan of GE offers women benefits equal to or greater than those offered to men. Both sexes are insured against the same risks. Sex-based discrimination "does not result simply because an employer's disability benefits plan is less than all inclusive."

A 1972 interpretive guideline issued by the Equal Employment Opportunity Commission (EEOC), nevertheless, asserts that disability insurance schemes that exclude disability on account of pregnancy or childbirth violate section 703(a). Although such guidelines promulgated by expert administrative agencies are generally entitled to some judicial deference in statutory construction, they are not conclusive. Here the EEOC guideline is entitled to little weight; it was issued eight years after enactment of the 1964 Civil Rights Act, is contrary to legislative history, and conflicts with its own earlier interpretation of section 703(a)(1).

> The concept of "discrimination," of course, was well known at the time of enactment of Title VII, having been associated with the Fourteenth Amendment for nearly a century, and carrying with it a long history of judicial construction. When Congress makes it unlawful for an employer to "discriminate . . . on the basis of sex . . .", without further explanation of its meaning, we should not readily infer that it meant something different than what the concept of discrimination has traditionally meant.

Dothard v. *Rawlinson*, 433 U.S. 321 (1977)

Facts: A woman was denied employment as an Alabama prison guard because she failed to meet the statutory requirements with respect to minimum height and weight—5 feet, 2 inches, and 120 pounds. Additionally, a prison regulation barred women from employment in "contact positions" requiring continual close supervision of male inmates in maximum security institutions. Suit was brought attacking both the statutory requirements as to height and weight and the regulation as violating the protection against sex discrimination in employment guaranteed by Title VII of the Civil Rights Act of 1964. A three-judge federal district court sustained both attacks.

Questions: (1) Do the statutory requirements of Alabama with respect to height and weight for prison guards discriminate on the basis of sex in contravention of Title VII? (2) Does the regulation barring the employment of women in contact positions in prisons violate Title VII?

Decision: Yes to the first question and no to the second. Opinion by Justice Stewart. Vote: 8–1 on the first question and 6–3 on the second, White, Brennan, and Marshall dissenting in part.

Reasons: Title VII prohibits artificial and unnecessary barriers to employment based on sex. The contested standards for height and weight discriminate against women and were not shown to be job-related. The standards operate to disqualify more than 41 percent of the female population but less than 1 percent of the male population from employment as prison guards. These statistics established a prima facie case of unlawful sex discrimination that was unrebutted by the state. It failed to show that the standards with respect to height and weight were related to a particular degree of strength necessary for employment as a prison guard. A bona fide test of strength, administered fairly, would not run afoul of Title VII. The record in this case, however, contains no job-related justification for the standards for height and weight; thus, their discriminatory effect on women makes them unlawful under Title VII.

The prohibition against the employment of women in contact positions in all-male maximum security institutions is sufficiently job-related to escape condemnation under Title VII. Section 703(e) of that title permits sex-based discrimination where sex "is a bona fide occupational qualification reasonably necessary to the normal operation of that particular business or enterprise." This exception was meant to be narrowly construed. Because the maximum security prisons of Alabama contain numerous unsegregated sex offenders and are rampant with violence, the challenged prohibition falls within the narrow ambit of the exception. A female prison guard occupying a contact position may be victimized by assaults from inmates because of her womanhood. These assaults would threaten the order and security of the entire institution and thus undermine the woman's capacity to perform as a guard. The "peculiarly inhospitable" environment in Alabama prisons makes maleness a bona fide occupational qualification for a contact position in its all-male maximum security institutions.

In a related decision concerning Title VII, *Hazelwood School District* v. *United States*, 433 U.S. 299 (1977), the Court held that the government generally establishes a prima facie case of an unlawful pattern or practice of racial discrimination in employment if it shows a threefold disparity between the percentage of blacks hired and the percentage of blacks in the relevant labor market.

Aliens

The Court has addressed the issue of discrimination against aliens on numerous occasions since 1971. Classifications drawn by a state on the basis of alienage survive constitutional scrutiny under the equal protection clause only if such classifications are necessary to the advancement of a compelling state interest.[62] In contrast, the federal government may generally[63] discriminate against aliens if there is any minimally rational basis for doing so.[64] This relaxed standard of judicial review is justified because of the plenary authority of Congress over naturalization and immigration and the need to accommodate federal treatment of aliens to a rapidly changing international environment.

This term, in *Fiallo v. Bell*, 430 U.S. 787 (1977), minimal judicial scrutiny was enlisted to sustain federal statutes that gave certain preferences in immigration status to mothers and their illegitimate children if either was a U.S. citizen or permanent resident alien, but denied corresponding preferences to fathers and their illegitimate children. At the same time, the Court enhanced the constitutional protection from state discrimination enjoyed by aliens; in *Nyquist v. Mauclet*, 432 U.S. 1 (1977), the Court held that a classification discriminating among aliens triggers strict judicial scrutiny if it is aimed at aliens and only aliens are harmed by it.

Fiallo v. Bell, 430 U.S. 787 (1977)

Facts: Under provisions of the Immigration and Nationality Act of 1952, 8 U.S. Code 1101(b)(1)(D), 1101(b)(2), preferential immigration status is granted to aliens who qualify as children or parents of U.S. citizens or lawful permanent residents. A preferred alien child or parent is allowed entry into the country without regard to

---

[62] The compelling state interest test was enunciated in Graham v. Richardson, 403 U.S. 365 (1971) (striking down a state statute requiring aliens but not citizens to satisfy a durational residency requirement as a condition of receiving welfare benefits), and followed in In re Griffiths, 413 U.S. 717 (1973) (invalidating a state statute disqualifying aliens from the practice of law), and Sugarman v. Dougall, 413 U.S. 634 (1973) (overturning a state civil service statute excluding aliens from appointment to any positions classified as competitive).

[63] But see Hampton v. Wong, 426 U.S. 88 (1976). There the Court invoked somewhat tortuous reasoning in subjecting treatment of aliens by the U.S. Civil Service Commission to more stringent standards of judicial review than would be imposed on Congress or the President.

[64] Mathews v. Diaz, 426 U.S. 67 (1976).

statutory immigration quotas, and, if related to a citizen, without obtaining a labor certification. The act, however, excludes preferential immigration status to illegitimate children with fathers in the United States and to fathers of illegitimate children who are citizens of the United States or permanent resident aliens. No corresponding disqualification attaches to illegitimate children of mothers in the United States or to mothers of illegitimate children having U.S. citizenship or permanent alien status.

Three sets of unwed natural fathers and their illegitimate children brought suit in federal district court challenging the constitutionality of sections 1101(b)(1)(D) and 1101(b)(2). They claimed that the statutory provisions discriminated on the basis of sex, illegitimacy, and marital status in violation of due process and invaded rights of privacy without constitutional justification. The district court upheld the statutes.

Question: Are the challenged provisions of the Immigration and Nationality Act unconstitutional?

Decision: No. Opinion by Justice Powell. Vote: 6–3, White, Brennan, and Marshall dissenting.

Reasons: Congress has uniquely broad powers over the admission of aliens, and decisions to expel or exclude aliens are largely immune from judicial review. The fact that the exercise of these powers may impinge on fundamental rights or discriminate against suspect classes does not justify departing from a relaxed standard of judicial scrutiny. Congress has drawn many distinctions in the Immigration and Nationality Act in furtherance of its objective "to provide some—but not all—families with relief from various immigration restrictions that would otherwise hinder reunification of the family in this country." In this connection,

> Congress obviously has determined that preferential status is not warranted for illegitimate children and their natural fathers, perhaps because of a perceived absence in most cases of close family ties as well as concern with the serious problems of proof that usually lurk in paternity determinations. . . . It is not the judicial role in cases of this sort to probe and test the justifications for the legislative decision.

Nyquist v. *Mauclet*, 432 U.S. 1 (1977)

Facts: A New York statute bars resident aliens from obtaining state financial assistance for higher education if they fail to declare their intention to seek U.S. citizenship as soon as they become eligible. Citizens and aliens who have either applied for citizenship or have stated an intention to apply when they become eligible qualify for assistance under the statute. A federal district court held that the statutory discrimination against resident aliens in the distribution of educational assistance violated the equal protection clause of the Fourteenth Amendment.

Question: Does the equal protection clause prohibit a state from discriminating against resident aliens who decline to affirm an intention to seek U.S. citizenship in distributing financial assistance for higher education?

Decision: Yes. Opinion by Justice Blackmun. Vote: 5–4, Burger, Stewart, Powell, and Rehnquist dissenting.

Reasons: State classifications on the basis of alienage are inherently suspect. They pass equal protection scrutiny only if they are precisely drawn and are necessary to the advancement of a substantial government interest. Although the statutory discrimination at issue does not disqualify all aliens, it is "directed at aliens and . . . only aliens are harmed by it." That is sufficient to trigger strict judicial scrutiny.

The state offers two justifications for the discrimination: (1) to encourage the naturalization of aliens, and (2) to enhance the educational level of prospective members of its electorate. The first reason fails because the federal government exercises exclusive control over immigration and naturalization. The second is also faulty because the state's objective of educating the electorate would not be frustrated by making all resident aliens eligible for financial assistance. "Resident aliens are obligated to pay their full share of the taxes that support the assistance programs. There thus is no real unfairness in allowing resident aliens an equal right to participate in programs to which they contribute on an equal basis."

Federal Courts and Procedure

As discussed in chapter 1, the Court expanded the reach of its abstention doctrine from criminal or quasi-criminal proceedings to civil proceedings in which the vindication of important state interests is implicated.[65] In *Juidice* v. *Vail*, 430 U.S. 327 (1977), the Court held

---

[65] Deriving from considerations of comity, the doctrine generally prohibits federal courts from enjoining pending state judicial proceedings on constitutional grounds at the behest of the state court defendant.

that federal courts must abstain from enjoining pending state civil contempt proceedings at the behest of the defendant unless he would otherwise suffer great and immediate irreparable harm. Also, in *Trainor v. Hernandez*, 431 U.S. 434 (1977), federal courts were instructed to apply the abstention doctrine to pending state civil suits seeking recovery of welfare monies wrongfully received. The primary reasons underlying the doctrine of abstention suggest that the Court will continue to bring additional types of suits within its embrace.[66]

The Court rejected a constitutional attack on the administrative procedures governing enforcement of the civil penalty provisions of the Occupational Safety and Health Act. Charged with violations, employers claimed a Seventh Amendment right to jury trial that attaches to suits at common law. By an 8–0 vote in *Atlas Roofing Co., Inc. v. Occupational Safety and Health Review Commission*, 430 U.S. 442 (1977), the Court disposed of the claim by reaffirming the longstanding rule that the enforcement of public rights in administrative proceedings does not trigger the protections of the Seventh Amendment.

An unrelenting caseload burden continues to plague the system of federal courts. [67] Time for oral argument has been reduced, and the use of uninformative per curiam opinions has grown; assembly-line justice threatens to invade the federal courts. With a crisis on the horizon, Congress finally seems disposed to heed the calls of the Chief Justice and others for legislative relief. The use of three-judge courts has been narrowly restricted.[68] There is a high probability that the 95th Congress will enact statutes to reduce diversity juris-

---

[66] Abstention is required, the Court has stated, to avoid interfering with the vindication of important state policies and casting negative inferences on the competence and willingness of state courts to enforce constitutional rights. The latter consideration will be present in most pending state court proceedings where the defendant has the opportunity to raise his constitutional claims as a defense. The former consideration is not easily cabined because states do not ordinarily rank the importance of particular public policies whether embodied in statutes or otherwise.

[67] See, for example, Remarks of Chief Justice Burger before the American Law Institute, Mayflower Hotel, Washington, D.C., May 17, 1977; and Address of Chief Judge Harry Phillips to the Sixth Circuit Judicial Conference and Address of Chief Judge Thomas E. Fairchild to the Seventh Circuit Judicial Conference, *The Third Branch* (a newsletter published by the Administrative Office of the U.S. Courts and the Federal Judicial Center), May 1977, pp. 3-4.

[68] See P.L. 94-381, 94th Congress, 1st session (1975) (generally eliminating three-judge courts, except for suits attacking the constitutionality of the apportionment of congressional districts or the apportionment of any statewide legislative body); P.L. 93-528, 93rd Congress, 2d session (1974) (eliminating three-judge courts in certain antitrust and Interstate Commerce Commission cases).

diction,[69] create more than 140 additional federal judgeships,[70] and expand the jurisdiction of federal magistrates.[71] A proposed National Court of Appeals[72] and a requirement that a judicial impact statement accompany each reported bill affecting the federal courts are less likely to receive congressional approval.

Reducing the caseloads of federal courts will advance the cause of justice in at least two important respects. First, speedier justice will prevent the wealthier litigants from obtaining unfair settlements at the expense of plaintiffs who need immediate financial relief. Equally important, federal adjudication will not be distorted by the fear of opening the floodgates to a new class of litigation. This fear may have influenced the decisions of the Court this term to deny indirect purchasers standing to sue for treble-damages based upon antitrust violations[73] and to exclude violations of corporate fiduciary duties from the antifraud provisions of the Securities Exchange Act.[74]

Juidice v. *Vail*, 430 U.S. 327 (1977)

Facts: Judgment debtors were threatened with imprisonment in pending state civil contempt proceedings. They obtained a federal district court injunction against enforcement of the state civil contempt statutes on constitutional grounds. The debtors had declined to assert their constitutional claims in the state court proceedings. State officials appealed, claiming that the federal court injunction violated the doctrine of abstention established in *Younger* v. *Harris*, 401 U.S. 37 (1971), and *Huffman* v. *Pursue, Ltd.*, 420 U.S. 592 (1975).

Question: Did the federal district court err in refusing to abstain from adjudicating the constitutionality of the state civil contempt statutes?

Decision: Yes. Opinion by Justice Rehnquist. Vote: 6–3, Brennan, Marshall, and Stewart dissenting.

---

[69] H.R. 761, 95th Congress, 1st session (1977).

[70] See S. 11, 95th Congress, 1st session (1977), which was approved by the Senate on May 24, 1977; H.R. 7843, as approved by the House on February 7, 1978, 124 Cong. Rec., February 7, 1978 (daily ed.) H717-733.

[71] See S. 1613, 95th Congress, 1st session (1977), which was approved by the Senate on July 22, 1977; H.R. 7493, 95th Congress, 1st session (1977).

[72] See H.R. 3969, 95th Congress, 1st session (1977).

[73] Illinois Brick v. Illinois, 431 U.S. 720 (1977).

[74] Santa Fe Industries, Inc. v. Green, 430 U.S. 462 (1977).

Reasons: In *Younger*, the Court enunciated a doctrine of abstention premised on a proper respect for the independence of states and state courts in the federalist system of the nation and their ability and willingness to enforce constitutional rights. *Younger* held that federal courts must abstain from enjoining pending state criminal proceedings on constitutional grounds unless the defendant proves that the proceedings would cause him great and immediate irreparable harm. Only in extraordinary circumstances can this burden of proof be met. *Huffman* extended the *Younger* doctrine to state civil proceedings both in aid of and closely related to criminal statutes, such as proceedings seeking the abatement of a civil nuisance. The guiding principle of *Younger* and *Huffman* is that application of the abstention doctrine extends to any pending state court proceeding that vindicates an important state interest—whether the proceeding is labeled civil, quasi-criminal, or criminal—and where federal intervention would reflect negatively on the ability of the state court to enforce constitutional rights.

> A State's interest in the contempt process, through which it vindicates the regular operation of its judicial system, so long as that system itself affords the opportunity to pursue federal claims within it, is surely an important interest. . . . The contempt power lies at the core of the administration of a State's judicial system.

In addition, the federal injunction in this case reflected a distrust of the ability and willingness of the state court to adjudicate constitutional claims. Thus, the *Younger* and *Huffman* abstention principles raised a bar to the federal court injunction against the pending civil contempt proceedings of the state absent proof of extraordinary circumstances. Such circumstances exist if the state proceeding is motivated by a desire to harass, is conducted in bad faith, or is pursuant to a flagrantly unconstitutional statute. None of these circumstances was either alleged or proved in the federal district court suit.

Trainor v. Hernandez, 431 U.S. 434 (1977)

Facts: Alleging that two recipients of welfare had fraudulently concealed assets in applying for and receiving public assistance, Illinois filed a civil suit seeking recovery of the monies wrongfully received. Concurrently, the state instituted attachment proceedings against money in the credit union account of the recipients. As authorized by state law, a writ of attachment freezing the account was issued automatically by the clerk of the court before the recipients were provided notice or an opportunity for a hearing. Declining to challenge the constitutionality of the attachment law in state court, the recipients obtained a federal district court injunction forbidding enforcement of the law on the ground that it patently violated procedural due process. The district court concluded that the abstention doctrine enunciated in *Younger* v. *Harris*, 401 U.S. 37 (1971), and its progeny did not require dismissal of the suit, because the questioned attachment law offered remedies to both private and public plaintiffs and was not intended to vindicate criminal or quasi-criminal interests of a state.

Question: Did the federal district court err in failing to dismiss the suit attacking the constitutionality of the state attachment law under the abstention doctrine of *Younger* v. *Harris*?

Decision: Yes. Opinion by Justice White. Vote: 5–4, Stewart, Brennan, Marshall, and Stevens dissenting.

Reasons: Generally speaking, questions of abstention arise when a plaintiff challenges the constitutionality of a state law in federal court after bypassing the opportunity to assert his claim as a defense in pending state court proceedings instituted by the state. In *Younger* v. *Harris* the Court held that federal court abstention is ordinarily required if the pending state proceeding is a criminal prosecution. *Younger* recognized an exception to this rule if the state prosecution threatens great and immediate irreparable injury to the federal plaintiff. The underlying rationale of *Younger* is that states should be permitted to effectuate important government interests—whether labeled criminal, quasi-criminal, or civil—without interference by a federal court that would reflect negatively on the ability and willingness of state courts to vindicate constitutional rights.

Here the state invoked the challenged attachment law as part of its civil suit to recover welfare payments alleged to have been fraudulently obtained. "Both the suit and the accompanying writ of garnishment were brought to vindicate important state policies such as safeguarding the fiscal integrity of [its public assistance] programs." The fraudulent conduct charged in the civil suit, moreover, is a crime under state law. In these circumstances, the sovereign state interests at stake in the proceedings to recover welfare benefits wrongfully obtained were sufficiently important to trigger application of the *Younger* abstention doctrine.

This case presents no extraordinary circumstances of the type recognized in *Younger* as justifying injunctions by federal courts.

There is no claim that the state suit was brought in bad faith or for the purpose of harassment. And the questioned state attachment law is not flagrantly and patently unconstitutional under the procedural due process holdings of *North Georgia Finishing, Inc.* v. *Di-Chem, Inc.*, 419 U.S. 601 (1975), and *Mitchell* v. *W. T. Grant Co.*, 416 U.S. 600 (1974). Abstention would not be required, however, if the federal plaintiffs were barred from asserting their due process claims in the pending state proceedings. The district court should consider this issue on remand.

Atlas Roofing Co., Inc. v. *Occupational Safety and Health Review Commission*, 430 U.S. 442 (1977)

Facts: The Occupational Safety and Health Act (OSHA) of 1970 requires employers to furnish employees with a working place free from recognized health or safety hazards and authorizes the secretary of labor to establish health and safety standards. OSHA empowers the secretary to obtain abatement orders and civil penalties of up to $10,000 for violation of a standard by means of an administrative proceeding before the three-member Occupational Safety and Health Review Commission. Commission orders are reviewable in the federal courts of appeal. Employers who had been ordered by the commission to pay civil penalties brought suit claiming that the enforcement procedures of OSHA violated the Seventh Amendment guarantee of a jury trial for suits at common law. Two courts of appeals rejected the claim.

Question: Does the Seventh Amendment prevent Congress from assigning to an administrative agency the task of adjudicating violations of OSHA?

Decision: No. Opinion by Justice White. Vote: 8–0. Blackmun did not participate.

Reasons: The Seventh Amendment guarantee of a jury trial applies only to "suits at common law." That phrase has been construed to encompass only cases tried prior to the adoption of the amendment in "courts of law in which jury trial was customary as distinguished from courts of equity or admiralty in which jury trial was not." In *Block* v. *Hirsh*, 256 U.S. 135 (1921), the Court established the general rule that the Seventh Amendment has no application to administrative proceedings in which jury trials would be incompatible with the whole concept of administrative adjudication.

In short, where "the Government sues in its sovereign capacity to enforce public rights created by statutes within the power of Congress to enact . . . the Seventh Amendment does not prohibit Congress from assigning the factfinding function and initial adjudication to an administrative forum with which the jury would be incompatible."

This general principle derives strength from the fact that when the Seventh Amendment was adopted, suits at common law could generally be tried by jury only when courts of law supplied both the cause of action and an adequate remedy. The amendment thus does not require a jury trial for the enforcement of public rights created by statute after its adoption.

Prisons and the Rights of Prisoners

Several dramatic prison riots and public concern with crime have brought issues concerning prisons and the rights of prisoners to the fore in this decade. At present, many prisons are intolerably overcrowded, rates of recidivism are high,[75] and no treatment program has proven to be effective in reducing these rates.[76] There is no consensus as to what changes in the existing administration of prisons or treatment of prisoners would yield net social benefits. Nevertheless, some innovative programs have been attempted in recent years. The federal Bureau of Prisons established grievance machinery in April 1974 that is resolving a large proportion of the complaints of prisoners.[77] The bureau is also offering a voluntary rehabilitation program patterned after the recommendations of Norval Morris[78] at its institution in Butner, North Carolina.[79] Connecticut, Minnesota, and Illinois are permitting private industry to train and employ workers in career jobs available outside the confines of

---

[75] Rates of recidivism generally range between 33 and 80 percent depending on how recidivism is defined (as a new arrest or a new conviction) and how many years after release are examined.

[76] See Robert Martinson, "What Works?—Questions and Answers about Prison Reform," *Public Interest*, no. 35 (Spring 1974).

[77] The grievance machinery handles approximately 13,000 complaints annually and grants some type of relief in approximately 20 percent of the cases. Its utility is reflected in part by the decrease in petitions filed by federal prisoners in U.S. district courts from 5,047 in fiscal 1975 to 4,780 in fiscal 1976. See Administrative Office of U.S. Courts, *Judicial Workload Statistics*, July-December 1976, p. 17.

[78] See Norval Morris, *The Future of Imprisonment* (Chicago: University of Chicago Press, 1974).

[79] The program commenced in April 1976.

prison.[80] The widespread failure and unfairness in the administration of parole has prompted Attorneys General Edward Levi and Griffin Bell to call for its replacement with a system assuring more certain and equitable punishment.[81] Legislation is pending in Congress that would limit the discretion of the U.S. Parole Commission in setting the time of a federal prisoner's release.[82]

These developments have emerged from considerable turmoil within prisons that has spawned a prodigious quantity of litigation,[83] with significant cases reaching the Supreme Court generally falling into three groups. The first group has raised troublesome issues concerning the internal administration of prisons, that is, prison security and rehabilitation of prisoners. In the absence of a consensus as to the hazards and benefits of particular prison rules and practices, the Court has been extremely reluctant to restrict the authority of prison administrators on constitutional grounds.[84] This term the Court held that prison officials have discretion to curtail the exercise of First Amendment rights by prisoners if the curtailment is rationally related to the protection of prison order and security. According to *Jones v. North Carolina Prisoners' Labor Union*, 433 U.S. 119 (1977), only if the fears of prison officials have been shown conclusively to be wrong, can restrictions on the First Amendment freedoms of prisoners be constitutionally overturned. The Court also gave prison administrators wide leeway in providing medical care. In *Estelle v. Gamble*, 429 U.S. 97 (1976), it held that the Eighth Amendment protection against cruel and unusual punishment requires only that prison doctors or guards not exhibit deliberate indifference to serious medical needs of prisoners.

A second category of suits in behalf of prisoners has concerned access to legal assistance and the courts. The general expertise of the Court in this area has supplied a confidence and resolve to strike

---

[80] See *Business Week*, July 18, 1977, p. 56.

[81] Address by Attorney General Levi before the Governor's Conference on Employment and the Prevention of Crime, Marc Plaza Hotel, Milwaukee, Wisconsin, Feb. 2, 1976; Testimony of Attorney General Bell, Hearings on S. 1437 before the Senate Judiciary Subcommittee on Criminal Laws and Procedure, 95th Congress, 1st session (1977).

[82] S. 1437, 95th Congress, 1st session (1977), as approved by the Senate on January 30, 1978, 124 Cong. Rec., January 30, 1978 (daily ed.) S860.

[83] In fiscal 1976, almost 20,000 petitions were filed by prisoners in federal district courts, a number equal to approximately 15 percent of the total number of civil filings, representing a tenfold increase since 1960. See Administrative Office of U.S. Courts, *1976 Annual Report of the Director*, p. 96.

[84] See, for example, Wolff v. McDonnell, 418 U.S. 539 (1974); Meachum v. Fano, 427 U.S. 215 (1976).

its own constitutional balance between the needs of prison security and the right to legal assistance. The balance has generally tilted in favor of the prisoner,[85] as it did this term in *Bounds* v. *Smith*, 430 U.S. 817 (1977), in which the Court recognized a prisoner's constitutional right of access to an adequate law library or comparable legal assistance.

The Court has confronted a third category of cases that raise questions concerning federal habeas corpus or collateral review of federal and state convictions. The grounds for attacking a conviction in federal habeas proceedings expanded continuously through the 1960s.[86] The Burger Court, however, has contracted the scope of federal habeas review,[87] spurred by the enormous growth of habeas litigation,[88] the practical difficulties of reviewing a conviction many years after it was rendered,[89] and a renewed respect for state rules of procedure and the competency of state courts.[90] This term, federal habeas review underwent further contraction in a decision in *Wainwright* v. *Sykes*, 433 U.S. 72 (1977), in which the Court declined to review a conviction based on an alleged involuntary confession because the prisoner had failed to comply with a state rule requiring contemporaneous objection to its admission at trial.

Jones v. *North Carolina Prisoners' Labor Union, Inc.*, 433 U.S. 119 (1977)

Facts: A prisoners' labor union composed of 2,000 North Carolina inmates was organized for the purpose of improving prison working conditions through collective bargaining. Thereafter, state officials issued regulations to prevent the expansion, formation, or operation of such unions. Pursuant to these regulations, prison officials prohibited inmates from soliciting other inmates to join the union, barred all union meetings, and refused to deliver bulk mailings

---

[85] See Wolff v. McDonnell, 418 U.S. 539 (1974); Procunier v. Martinez, 416 U.S. 396 (1974).

[86] See, for example, Kaufman v. United States, 394 U.S. 217 (1969); Fay v. Noia, 372 U.S. 391 (1963).

[87] See Davis v. United States, 411 U.S. 233 (1973); Francis v. Henderson, 425 U.S. 536 (1976); Stone v. Powell, 428 U.S. 465 (1976).

[88] More than 9,200 habeas corpus petitions were filed in federal district courts in fiscal 1976, an increase of 45 percent over the number filed in 1966. See Administrative Office of U.S. Courts, *1976 Annual Report of the Director*, p. 94.

[89] See Wainwright v. Sykes, 433 U.S. 72 (1977).

[90] See notes 87 and 89, above. See also Younger v. Harris, 401 U.S. 37 (1971); Kugler v. Helfant, 421 U.S. 117 (1975).

from and concerning the union for redistribution among inmates. The union brought suit under 42 U.S. Code 1983 alleging that the restrictions on the organizing activities of prisoners' unions violated First Amendment rights of free speech and association and the equal protection clause of the Fourteenth Amendment. A federal district court held that the ban on solicitation violated the First Amendment because there was no evidence that the union had been used to disrupt prison operations. It concluded that the ban on union meetings and the denial of bulk-mailing privileges violated the equal protection clause, because the Jaycees and Alcoholics Anonymous were not similarly restricted in their prison activities.

Question: Are the contested North Carolina restrictions on the formation and operation of prisoners' unions constitutional?

Decision: Yes. Opinion by Justice Rehnquist. Vote: 7–2, Brennan and Marshall dissenting.

Reasons: The First Amendment rights of a prison inmate are restricted to those that are consistent with his status as a prisoner and with legitimate penological objectives. Because of the complexities of prison administration, federal courts should give great deference to prison officials in determining whether particular restrictions on the First Amendment rights of prisoners are justified.

Here state prison officials testified that the formation of labor unions of prisoners was fraught with potential dangers. They might increase friction between inmates and prison personnel and between members and nonmembers of the unions. Unions could acquire an influence over inmates that might lead to work stoppages, riots, and chaos. The prohibitions against solicitation of inmates and union meetings was rationally related to avoidance of this potential disruption of prison operations.

The restraints on free speech and association imposed by the antiunion regulations are minimal. The denial of bulk-mailing privileges requires the union to pay higher mailing rates but places no limits on what it chooses to communicate. The denial is necessary to prevent the smuggling of contraband in bulk deliveries. The prohibition on solicitation and group meetings of the union are no broader than necessary to protect order and security within prisons. The rights of free speech and association of inmates curtailed by the prohibitions are constitutional if correctional officials, in the exercise of informed discretion, reasonably conclude that the curtailment is necessary to prevent disruption or interference with legitimate penological objectives. Restrictions on First Amendment activity may be imposed before the "eve of a riot." The discretion of prison officials should not be overturned unless their fears have been shown conclusively to be wrong. Such proof was lacking in this case.

The equal protection claim also lacks merit. A prison is not a public forum where discrimination against particular types of protected speech is constitutionally disfavored. Thus, the preferential treatment accorded the Jaycees and Alcoholics Anonymous passes constitutional scrutiny if it is rationally based. That test is clearly satisfied. Both groups were allowed to hold meetings within the prison and to exercise bulk-mailing privileges because they serve a rehabilitative purpose consistent with the goals and desires of prison administrators. Unlike prisoner labor unions, they pose no threat to prison order or security. These reasons satisfactorily explain the preferential treatment accorded the Jaycees and Alcoholics Anonymous.

Estelle v. *Gamble*, 429 U.S. 97 (1976)

Facts: Alleging inadequate treatment of a back injury, a Texas state inmate brought suit under 42 U.S. Code 1983 [91] against a prison medical officer, the prison warden, and the director of the state department of corrections. He claimed that despite his examination by prison medical personnel seventeen times during a three-month interval and the receipt of extensive drug treatment, the failure to use other treatments or to provide additional diagnoses to cure his back pain constituted cruel and unusual punishment in violation of the Eighth Amendment. The district court dismissed the complaint. The court of appeals reversed, reasoning that the allegations of inadequate medical treatment and improper diagnosis stated a valid Eighth Amendment claim.

Question: Did the inmate's complaint allege a valid Eighth Amendment claim under 42 U.S. Code 1983?

Decision: No. Opinion by Justice Marshall. Vote: 8–1, Stevens dissenting.

Reasons: The Eighth Amendment, as interpreted in *Trop* v. *Dulles*, 356 U.S. 86 (1958), and *Gregg* v. *Georgia*, 428 U.S. 153 (1976), proscribes punishments inconsistent with contemporary civilized standards of decency or involving the unnecessary and wanton

---

[91] That section authorizes suits for violations of constitutional rights committed under color of state law.

infliction of pain. Under these standards, the government is constitutionally obliged "to provide medical care for those whom it is punishing by incarceration."

> Deliberate indifference to serious medical needs of prisoners constitutes the "unnecessary and wanton infliction of pain" . . . proscribed by the Eighth Amendment. This is true whether the indifference is manifested by prison doctors in their response to the prisoner's needs or by prison guards in intentionally denying or delaying access to medical care or intentionally interfering with the treatment once prescribed.

The test of deliberate indifference, however, is not satisfied by claims of medical malpractice or inadequate medical treatment. A cognizable Eighth Amendment claim based on prison medical treatment requires allegations of "acts or omissions sufficiently harmful to evidence deliberate indifference to serious medical needs." In this case, the *pro se* complaint of the prisoner, construed liberally as required by *Haines* v. *Kerner*, 404 U.S. 519 (1972), at best alleges only medical malpractice. Accordingly, it failed to state a valid Eighth Amendment claim against the prison doctors.

The Court remanded the case for determination of whether the allegations stated a valid claim against either the warden or the director of the department of corrections under the deliberate indifference test.

Bounds v. *Smith*, 430 U.S. 817 (1977)

Facts: Inmates of a state penal institution brought suit in federal district court claiming an unconstitutional denial of the right of access to the courts because of the absence of an adequate prison law library or other legal assistance. Relying on *Younger* v. *Gilmore*, 404 U.S. 15 (1971), the district court upheld the claim and ordered state officials to devise a program that would assure inmates constitutionally adequate access to the courts. The officials proposed to establish seven comprehensive law libraries in conveniently located prisons across the state and smaller libraries in a segregation unit and a women's prison. The libraries would stock legal forms, writing paper, and other equipment needed in the preparation of legal documents. Inmates would be trained as research assistants to aid other inmates, who would be transported to one of the law libraries on request. The proposal did not provide for attorneys or independent legal advisers for inmates. The district court approved the state proposal as constitutionally adequate, and the court of appeals affirmed, except insofar as the library plan denied female inmates the same rights of access as men.

Question: Was the law library plan of the district court, as modified by the court of appeals, constitutionally required to protect the inmates' right of access to the courts?

Decision: Yes. Opinion by Justice Marshall. Vote: 6–3, Burger, Stewart, and Rehnquist dissenting.

Reasons: For decades, the Court has recognized that prisoners have a constitutional right of access to the courts. In *Younger v. Gilmore*, the Court held that state authorities have an affirmative constitutional duty to assure that this right is implemented. If attorneys or other legal assistance is not provided, the availability of an adequate library is essential to the preparation of habeas corpus petitions or civil rights complaints. Experience has shown that prisoners are capable of making significant use of law libraries. "We hold, therefore, that the fundamental constitutional right of access to the courts requires prison authorities to assist inmates in the preparation and filing of meaningful legal papers by providing prisoners with adequate law libraries or adequate assistance from persons trained in the law."

The Court observed that as alternatives to law libraries, prison officials might assure inmates meaningful access to the courts through the use of prisoners trained as paralegals and supervised by attorneys, law students, or the offices of public defender legal services organizations.

Wainwright v. *Sykes*, 433 U.S. 72 (1977)

Facts: A Florida state prisoner sought federal habeas corpus relief under 28 U.S. Code 2254 on the ground that his trial was constitutionally tainted by the admission of an involuntary confession. No objection to the confession had been raised during trial or appeal. State courts declined to entertain the federal habeas claim in state collateral proceedings seeking to overturn the prisoner's conviction. Their rulings were premised on a state rule of procedure that requires a defendant to make contemporaneous objection at trial to the admission of involuntary confessions. The failure of the prisoner to comply with that rule constituted a waiver of his rights under state law. Nevertheless, the federal district court held that the failure did not bar assertion of the claim of involuntariness in federal habeas proceedings, and it upheld the claim on the merits. The court of appeals affirmed, reasoning that under *Fay v. Noia,* 372 U.S. 391 (1963), the failure to comply with a state rule of procedure for advancing a constitutional claim would prevent federal habeas review of the claim only if the rule had been flouted deliberately for reasons having to do with trial tactics.

Question: Where a defendant fails to comply with a legitimate state rule of procedure for raising constitutional claims, does 28 U.S. Code 2254 nevertheless require consideration of the claims in a federal habeas corpus proceeding if the rule was not deliberately bypassed for tactical purposes?

Decision: No. Opinion by Justice Rehnquist. Vote: 7–2, Brennan and Marshall dissenting.

Reasons: Generally speaking, 28 U.S. Code 2254 authorizes review of all constitutional claims raised by state prisoners in federal habeas corpus proceedings. Considerations of comity and concerns about the orderly administration of criminal justice, however, justify limited exceptions to this rule. In *Francis v. Henderson,* 425 U.S. 536 (1976), a state defendant failed to make a pretrial challenge to the composition of a grand jury as required by state procedures. The Court held that the failure precluded a belated constitutional attack on the grand jury in federal habeas proceedings absent a showing of cause for the noncompliance and actual prejudice resulting from the alleged constitutional violation. The *Francis* rule should also apply in this case.

The Florida contemporaneous-objection rule advances several interests: it enables a determination of the constitutional claim when memories are freshest; if the claim is upheld and the questioned evidence excluded, it contributes to finality in criminal litigation; and, if the evidence is admitted after a full hearing, the state ruling will offer considerable guidance in federal habeas proceedings. Permitting wholesale departures from the contemporaneous-objection rule, moreover, may encourage sandbagging by defense lawyers, who may risk a verdict of guilty in state court in hopes of obtaining federal habeas corpus relief if the gamble is unsuccessful. Procedural rules that encourage error-free trials are thoroughly desirable, and the contemporaneous-objection rule falls within this category.

The "cause" and "prejudice" exception of the *Francis* rule will afford an adequate guarantee, we think, that the rule will not prevent a federal habeas court from adjudicating for the first time the federal constitutional claim of a defendant who in the absence of such an adjudication will be the victim of a miscarriage of justice.

The sweeping, deliberate bypass language of *Fay* v. *Noia* is rejected as the general test for determining whether the failure of a defendant to comply with a state rule of procedure in asserting a constitutional claim precludes assertion of the claim in federal habeas proceedings.

Moody v. *Daggett*, 429 U.S. 78 (1976)

Facts: After a federal parolee had been convicted and imprisoned for federal crimes committed while on parole, the United States Board of Parole lodged a parole violator warrant with prison officials. The unexecuted warrant was tantamount to a detainer and assured that the parolee would not be released from custody until the board had determined whether his parole should be revoked. The board denied the request of the parolee that the warrant be executed promptly and expressed an intent to delay execution of it until after his release from prison. The parolee brought suit seeking dismissal of the warrant on the ground that a prompt hearing concerning revocation of his parole was constitutionally required. (An immediate revocation of parole would have permitted the two sentences of the parolee to run concurrently.) The district court dismissed the suit and the court of appeals affirmed.

Question: Is a fedaral parolee imprisoned for crimes committed while on parole constitutionally entitled to a prompt hearing concerning revocation of his parole?

Decision: No. Opinion by Chief Justice Burger. Vote: 7–2, Brennan and Stevens dissenting.

Reasons: In *Morrissey* v. *Brewer*, 408 U.S. 471 (1972), the Court held that the conditional freedom of a parolee was a liberty interest protected by the due process clause of the Fourteenth Amendment and could not be revoked absent specified procedural safeguards. In this case, however, no liberty interest of the parolee is threatened by the failure of the board to execute its warrant promptly. The existing confinement of the parolee is the result of two criminal convictions. If the board revokes his parole after completion of his second sentence, it has power to grant, retroactively, the equivalent of concurrent sentences. Finally, even assuming a constitutionally protected liberty interest in the grant of parole, the unexecuted warrant does not prejudice the opportunity for parole on the second sentence. During a parole hearing, the parolee will have "the same full opportunity to persuade the [board] that he should be released from federal custody as [he] would [have during] an immediate hearing on the parole violator warrant."

Labor Law

Approximately 25 percent of the work force of the United States belongs to labor unions. The significant issues of labor law decided by the Supreme Court frequently affect the relative strength of business and labor in the collective-bargaining process and are often spawned by disputes over collective-bargaining agreements. Evaluated from this perspective, the 1976–1977 term reflected a mixed record of triumphs and defeats for unions.

Seniority systems established by collective-bargaining agreements are central to union power. In two cases, attacks were lodged against seniority systems under Title VII of the Civil Rights Act of 1964. In one case, *International Brotherhood of Teamsters* v. *United States*, 431 U.S. 324 (1977), it was claimed that a seniority system that perpetuated the effects of past racial discrimination was illegal. In the other, *Trans World Airlines, Inc.* v. *Hardison*, 432 U.S. 63 (1977), adherence by an employer to seniority provisions was claimed to constitute religious discrimination insofar as it required a member of the Worldwide Church of God to perform Saturday work. Both attacks on the seniority systems were rejected. In contrast, in *N.L.R.B.* v. *Pipefitters*, 429 U.S. 507 (1977), the Court rebuffed a union claim that striking in order to force compliance with a collective-bargaining agreement was immune from condemnation as a secondary boycott under the National Labor Relations Act. This decision sharply undercut union power to preserve jobs at construction sites.[92]

The ability of unions to launch successful strikes against employers was further undercut in two other decisions. In *Ohio Bureau of Employment Services* v. *Hodory*, 431 U.S. 471 (1977), the Court upheld the authority of states to deny unemployment benefits to a worker who was laid off because of a labor dispute, except in in-

---

[92] In 1951, the Court circumscribed the right of construction employees to strike by condemning "common situs" picketing as an unlawful secondary boycott under the National Labor Relations Act. N.L.R.B. v. Denver Bldg. & Construction Trades Council, 341 U.S. 675 (1951).

stances in which the employer had ordered a lockout. Similarly, denial by a state of welfare benefits to workers whose unemployment was the result of a strike was sustained in *Batterton* v. *Francis*, 432 U.S. 416 (1977).

In a case arising out of the internal politics of a union, *United Steelworkers of America, Local 3489* v. *Usery*, 429 U.S. 305 (1977), the Court invalidated a rule that restricted eligibility for office in a local union to those who had attended 50 percent of the meetings of the local union over the preceding three-year period.

Trans World Airlines, Inc. v. *Hardison*, 432 U.S. 63 (1977)

Facts: Section 703(a)(1) of the Civil Rights Act of 1964, as amended, prohibits discrimination against employees on the basis of religion. It requires employers to "reasonably accommodate" an employee's religious observance or practice unless the accommodation would impose "undue hardship on the conduct of the employer's business." Hardison, an adherent of the Worldwide Church of God, was discharged by Trans World Airlines (TWA) for refusing, as his religious faith required, to work on Saturdays. A federal district court rejected Hardison's claim that the discharge violated section 703(a)(1). It found that Hardison's job was essential on weekends, that his avoidance of Saturday work would violate the seniority provisions of TWA's collective-bargaining contract, that filling his position with other regular employees would leave other Saturday operations undermanned, and that premium wages would be required to employ someone not regularly assigned Saturday work. The court of appeals reversed. It concluded that TWA had rejected three reasonable ways of accommodating Hardison's religious beliefs: (1) permitting him to work a four-day week and utilizing other employees on Saturdays, (2) offering premium pay to employees who would work Saturdays in lieu of Hardison, and (3) seeking a variance from the seniority provisions of its collective-bargaining contract.

Questions: Did TWA violate section 703(a)(1) by failing to reasonably accommodate Hardison's religious beliefs without undue hardship?

Decision: No. Opinion by Justice White. Vote: 7–2, Brennan and Marshall dissenting.

Reasons: TWA made several efforts to accommodate Hardison's religious beliefs consistent with the seniority provisions of its collective-bargaining contract. It searched for a job not requiring Saturday work, it authorized a union steward to seek a swap of shifts, and it permitted Hardison's observance of special religious holidays. Adherence to a bona fide seniority system that works a discrimination on the basis of religion does not violate section 703(a)(1) unless the system has a discriminatory purpose. Here no discriminatory purpose was alleged. Accordingly, "TWA was not required by [section 703(a)(1)] to carve out a special exception to its seniority system in order to help Hardison to meet his religious obligations."

In addition, the three alternatives suggested by the court of appeals would involve costs to TWA in the form of lost efficiencies or higher wages. Requiring an employer to bear more than a *de minimus* cost to accommodate religious practices is an undue hardship. Thus, TWA had no obligation under section 703(a)(1) to incur these costs in order to give Hardison the privilege of avoiding Saturday work.

N.L.R.B. v. *Enterprise Association of Steam, Hot Water, Hydraulic Sprinkler, Pneumatic Tube, Ice Machine and General Pipefitters of New York and Vicinity, Local Union No. 638,* 429 U.S. 507 (1977)

Facts: Section 8(b)(4)(B) of the National Labor Relations Act prohibits a union from inducing employees to refuse to handle a company's goods or products when an objective of the inducement is to force an employer to cease doing business with the company. The section also provides, however, that it does not "make unlawful, where not otherwise unlawful, any primary strike or primary picketing." The National Labor Relations Board and the judiciary have construed secton 8(b)(4)(B) to prohibit only secondary, rather than primary, strikes and picketing.

A general contractor on a housing project (Austin) awarded a subcontract to Hudik to perform heating, ventilation, and air-conditioning work. Hudik's employees were represented by a plumbing and pipefitting union (Enterprise). The subcontract provided that Hudik would install climate-control units manufactured by Slant/Fin. The internal piping was to be cut, threaded, and installed at a Slant/Fin factory. The Hudik-Enterprise collective-bargaining agreement, however, provided that all pipe threading and cutting would be performed on the job site. Enterprise refused to install the Slant/Fin units on the ground that internal piping was union work under its contract with Hudik. Austin filed an unfair labor practice complaint with the National Labor Relations Board on the theory that Enterprise violated section 8(b)(4)(B) by inducing its members to cease handling Slant/Fin units with the objective of forcing Austin to terminate its business with Slant/Fin.

The board upheld the complaint. Reasoning that Hudik lacked power to change the terms of the subcontract, the board concluded that the boycott of Slant/Fin units by the union was secondary because it sought to change the business relations of Austin. The court of appeals reversed.

Question: Did the refusal of the union to handle Slant/Fin units constitute an unfair labor practice under section 8(b)(4)(B)?

Decision: Yes. Opinion by Justice White. Vote: 6–3, Brennan, Stewart, and Marshall dissenting.

Reasons: Under *Local 1976, United Brotherhood of Carpenters* v. *N.L.R.B.*, 357 U.S. 93 (1958), the refusal of a union to handle goods for the purpose of enforcing a collective-bargaining contract is not necessarily immunized from challenge under section 8(b)(4)(B). That section may be violated where a union engages in a product boycott that has as one of its objectives the exertion of pressure against a secondary, as opposed to a primary, employer. The objectives of a product boycott must be determined in light of the totality of circumstances.

Here Enterprise sought to enforce its contract with Hudik by boycotting Slant/Fin climate-control units. Because Hudik lacked power unilaterally to change its subcontract, the work objectives of the union could be obtained only by exerting pressure on Austin to cease dealing with Slant/Fin.

> That the union may also have been seeking to enforce its contract and to convince Hudik that it should bid on no more jobs where prepiped units were specified does not alter the fact that the union refused to install the Slant/Fin units and asserted that the piping work on the [housing project] belonged to its members.

In these circumstances, the board could properly infer that the boycott of Slant/Fin units had the objective of influencing Austin in a manner prohibited by section 8(b)(4)(B).

Ohio Bureau of Employment Services v. *Hodory*, 431 U.S. 471 (1977)

Facts: An Ohio statute disqualifies for unemployment benefits persons whose unemployment is "due to a labor dispute other than a lockout at any factory . . . owned or operated by the employer by which he is or was last employed." A steel company employee who was furloughed because of a mine workers' strike that interrupted the supply of coal at his plant was denied benefits under the statute. He brought suit in federal district court claiming that the statute was pre-empted by federal unemployment laws and contravened the equal protection clause of the Fourteenth Amendment insofar as it disqualified persons lacking any responsibility for their unemployment. The district court sustained the equal protection challenge.

Question: Is the Ohio unemployment compensation statute either pre-empted by federal unemployment laws or unconstitutional under the equal protection clause?

Decision: No. Opinion by Justice Blackmun. Vote: 8–0. Rehnquist did not participate.

Reasons: The Social Security Act, 42 U.S. Code 501, requires state unemployment programs qualifying for federal funds to pay benefits "when due." Its legislative history shows that Congress intended to authorize qualifying state programs to exclude persons whose unemployment was caused by a labor dispute that they opposed or was otherwise beyond their control. The Ohio unemployment statute does not conflict with the objectives of the act and thus is not pre-empted simply because innocent persons are denied benefits.

The equal protection argument is likewise without merit. Because the challenged statute has to do with economics and social welfare and burdens no fundamental rights, it satisfies equal protection scrutiny if a rational basis can be found for its enactment. Ohio imposes taxes on private employers to support its unemployment compensation fund. An employer's tax rate varies according to the benefits paid to his eligible employees. The challenged statute achieves a rough justice by relieving an employer from increased unemployment taxes that would otherwise be triggered by paying benefits to his employees who are out of work because of a labor dispute other than a lockout ordered by the employer. In addition, the disqualification provision of the statute advances the legitimate state interests in the fiscal integrity of its unemployment compensation fund and in maintaining state neutrality in strikes called by unions. This satisfies the rationality required by the equal protection clause.

Batterton v. Francis, 432 U.S. 416 (1977)

Facts: Title IV of the Social Security Act establishes a federally assisted program of Aid to Families with Dependent Children (AFDC). Participating states with programs meeting federal standards receive AFDC matching funds to assist children who are needy because of the death, absence, or incapacity of a parent. In addition, states have the option under Title IV of adopting an AFDC-UF program to assist dependent children who are needy because of a father's unemployment. Acting pursuant to express statutory authority, the secretary of health, education, and welfare issued a regulation defining the term *unemployed father* for purposes of the AFDC-UF program. It permits participating states to exclude from the definition "a father whose unemployment results from participation in a labor dispute or who is unemployed by reason of conduct or circumstances which result or would result in disqualification for unemployment compensation under the State's unemployment compensation law." Exercising its option under the regulation, Maryland denied AFDC-UF benefits to families in which the fathers were ineligible for unemployment compensation because their unemployment was caused by a strike or misconduct. Suing in federal district court, the ineligible families attacked the validity of the HEW regulation on the ground that it lacked statutory authorization under Title IV. The district court sustained the attack. The court of appeals affirmed.

Question: Did Title IV authorize the challenged HEW regulation offering states discretion in defining unemployed fathers for purposes of the AFDC-UF program?

Decision: Yes. Opinion by Justice Blackmun. Vote: 5–4, White, Brennan, Marshall, and Stevens dissenting.

Reasons: "Congress . . . expressly delegated to the Secretary the power to prescribe standards for determining what constitutes 'unemployment' for purposes of AFDC-UF eligibility." The contested regulation is invalid only if it exceeds this statutory authority or if it constitutes an abuse of discretion.

The concept of unemployment is frequently limited to persons who are actively seeking work or whose unemployment is involuntary. Department of Labor statistics and state unemployment compensation programs often embrace such concepts of unemployment. "By allowing the States to exclude persons who would be disqualified under the State's unemployment compensation law, the Secretary has incorporated a well known and widely applied standard for 'unemployment.' " It represents a reasonable exercise of his statutory authority. Although the legislative history is ambiguous, Title IV was not intended to require the AFDC-UF program to have a uniform definition of unemployment throughout the United States.

United Steelworkers of America, Local 3489 v. Usery, 429 U.S. 305 (1977)

Facts: The constitution of the Steelworkers' International generally limits eligibility for local union office to only those members who have attended at least 50 percent of the regular local union meetings held during the three years preceding the election. The secretary of labor brought suit to invalidate a local election on the ground that the eligibility restriction violated section 401(c) of the Labor-Management Reporting and Disclosure Act of 1959 (LMRDA). That section provides in pertinent part that "every [union] member in good standing shall be eligible to be a candidate and to hold office" subject to "reasonable qualifications uniformly imposed." Although the contested restriction disqualified 96 percent of the members of the local union from candidacy, the union claimed that it was a "reasonable qualification" designed to encourage attendance at union meetings and to attract well-informed candidates. A court of appeals condemned the restriction as unreasonable under section 401(c).

Question: Does the challenged eligibility restriction that disqualifies more than 96 percent of union members as candidates for union office violate section 401(c)?

Decision Yes. Opinion by Justice Brennan. Vote: 6–3, Powell, Stewart, and Rehnquist dissenting.

Reasons: The basic objective of section 401(c) and related provisions in the LMRDA is to assure free and democratic elections. Restraints on potential corruption, abuse, or other wrongdoing by union officials are to be imposed by union members through exercise of "common sense and judgment in casting their ballots." These objectives are plainly undermined by a provision that excludes more than 96 percent of union members from union office.

It is argued that the provision is reasonable because a member can qualify for candidacy by attending only eighteen short meetings over a three-year period. But

> in the absense of a permanent "opposition party" within the union, opposition to the incumbent leadership is likely to emerge in response to particular issues at different times,

and member interest in changing union leadership is therefore likely to be at its highest only shortly before elections. Thus it is probable that to require that a member decide upon a candidacy at least 18 months in advance of an election when no issues exist to prompt that decision may not foster but discourage candidacies and to that extent impair the general membership's freedom to oust incumbents in favor of new leadership.

The reasonableness of the candidacy restriction cannot be sustained on the theory that it encourages attendance at union meetings, because it failed to improve attendance, and since a major premise of section 401(c) is that members are capable of evaluating candidates for union office, an eligibility restriction imposed for the purpose of seeking to preselect the best-informed candidates cannot qualify as reasonable.

Federal Regulation of Business: Antitrust, Securities, and Environmental Law

Plaintiffs departed from the Supreme Court empty-handed in six significant antitrust and securities cases this term. Decisions in two antitrust cases raised the quantum of proof necessary to establish an antitrust violation and circumscribed the types of plaintiffs with standing to seek damages for such infractions.

The Court replaced a ten-year-old rule [93] that automatically condemned territorial or customer restrictions on the resale of goods or services with a rule of reason in *Continental T.V., Inc. v. GTE Sylvania, Inc.*, 433 U.S. 36 (1977). It repudiated the view that vertical territorial or customer restrictions on the marketing of franchised products are universally anticompetitive, noting their potential for increasing interbrand competition. This procompetitive potential, the Court reasoned, justifies evaluating vertical territorial or customer restraints under the rule of reason. That standard would permit such vertical restraints if, in the light of all the circumstances, they tended to promote rather than destroy competition.

Consumers suffered a setback in *Illinois Brick Co. v. Illinois*, 431 U.S. 720 (1977), in which the Court held that indirect purchasers injured by antitrust violations are generally precluded from recovering treble damages for illegal overcharges under section 4 of the Clayton Act.[94] This decision insulates most manufacturers from the

---

[93] See United States v. Arnold, Schwinn & Co., 388 U.S. 365 (1967).
[94] The Court opined that indirect purchasers may recover treble damages when overcharges are passed on through a cost-plus contract or when they own or control a direct purchaser.

threat of consumer class-action treble-damage suits built on horizontal price-fixing conspiracies. At present, Congress is considering legislation to overturn the *Illinois Brick* rule and thereby authorize recovery of damages by both direct and indirect victims of antitrust violations.[95]

Treble-damage plaintiffs were also rebuffed in *Brunswick Corp. v. Pueblo Bowl-O-Mat, Inc.*, 429 U.S. 477 (1977), and *U.S. Steel Corp. v. Fortner Enterprises, Inc.*, 429 U.S. 610 (1977). In the former, a unanimous Court held that section 4 of the Clayton Act authorizes recovery of damages only for injuries of the type that the antitrust laws were designed to prevent, not those having only a *but for* causal link to an antitrust violation. In the latter, the Court overturned a finding of a lower court that U.S. Steel possessed sufficient power in the credit markets to taint an agreement tying the sale of its prefabricated homes to the use of its credit under the Sherman Act.

The Court continued its trend of recent terms to circumscribe application of the federal securities laws.[96] It refused in *Piper Aircraft Corp. v. Chris-Craft Industries, Inc.*, 430 U.S. 1 (1977), to imply a private damage action for tender offerors injured either by misleading statements made in violation of the Williams Act or by manipulation of the market as proscribed by Rule 10b-6 authorized by the Securities Exchange Act. It also rejected, in *Santa Fe Industries, Inc. v. Green*, 430 U.S. 462 (1977), an attempt to invoke Rule 10b-5 to police the fiduciary duties that majority shareholders owe to the minority.

In an important environmental decision, in *E.I. Du Pont de Nemours and Co. v. Train*, 430 U.S. 112 (1977), the Court sustained the authority of the Environmental Protection Agency to impose industrywide, as opposed to plant-by-plant, limitations on the discharge of water pollutants. The Court also held that new plants were barred from obtaining variances from the effluent limits under the Federal Water Pollution Control Act.

Continental T.V., Inc. v. *GTE Sylvania, Inc.*, 433 U.S. 36 (1977)

Facts: GTE Sylvania manufactures and sells television sets. It adopted a new marketing technique in 1962 after its share of the

---

[95] See H.R. 8359, 95th Congress, 1st session (1977); S. 1874, 95th Congress, 1st session (1977).

[96] See Reliance Electric Co. v. Emerson Electric Co., 404 U.S. 418 (1972); Kern County Land Co. v. Occidental Petroleum Corp., 411 U.S. 582 (1973); Blue Chip Stamps v. Manor Drug Stores, 427 U.S. 723 (1975); United Housing Foundation, Inc. v. Forman, 421 U.S. 837 (1975); Ernst & Ernst v. Hochfelder, 425 U.S. 185 (1976); Foremost-McKesson, Inc. v. Provident Securities Co., 423 U.S. 232 (1976).

market dropped to between 1 and 2 percent of national sales. To attract an aggressive group of franchised retail dealers, Sylvania required each franchisee to sell its television sets only from the location at which he was franchised. In 1965, after Sylvania had obtained a 5 percent share of national television sales, it canceled the franchise of Continental for violating the location restriction. In litigation between the two companies, Continental sought treble damages against Sylvania on the theory that the location restriction violated section 1 of the Sherman Act.[97] Relying on *United States* v. *Arnold, Schwinn & Co.,* 388 U.S. 365 (1967), the district court instructed the jury that any attempt by Sylvania to enforce the location restriction provision after having sold its television sets to franchisees would constitute a per se violation of section 1. The jury found in favor of Continental and awarded $1.7 million in treble damages.

The court of appeals reversed. It noted that *Schwinn* had condemned contracts restricting the territories or customers to whom franchised distributors or retailers could sell products as per se violations of section 1. Location restrictions, however, should be judged under the rule of reason, the court of appeals concluded, because they have less potential for competitive harm than territorial or customer restrictions.

Question: Under section 1 of the Sherman Act, should agreements between manufacturers and distributors that impose territorial, customer, or location restrictions on the sale of goods or services all be judged under the rule of reason and should *Schwinn* therefore be overruled?

Decision: Yes. Opinion by Justice Powell. Vote: 6–2, Brennan and Marshall dissenting.

Reasons: Section 1 of the Sherman Act prohibits only unreasonable restraints of trade or commerce. Ordinarily, the reasonableness of a restraint depends on an evaluation of all the circumstances to determine whether it tends to promote or destroy competition. As stated in *Northern Pac. R. Co.* v. *United States,* 356 U.S. 1 (1958), however, there are some practices, such as price fixing, "which because of their pernicious effect on competition and lack of any redeeming virtue are conclusively presumed to be unreasonable and therefore illegal without elaborate inquiry as to the precise harm they have caused or the business excuse for their use." *Schwinn* erred in concluding that vertical territorial or customer restrictions

---

[97] Section 1 prohibits contracts or conspiracies that unreasonably restrain trade in interstate commerce.

on the marketing of franchised products are universally anticompetitive. The reduction in intrabrand competition caused by such restrictions may be outweighed in some circumstances by their favorable effect on interbrand competition. New manufacturers can use vertical restraints to induce competent and aggressive retailers to invest the capital and labor required to distribute products unknown to the consumer. The good will of a manufacturer often depends on the availability and quality of service and repairs offered by the dealer. Vertical restraints may be necessary to create economic incentives for dealers to provide service of high quality. Because of the substantial scholarly and judicial authority supporting their economic utility, vertical restrictions should be tested under the rule of reason. That rule can adequately police particular vertical restraints having anticompetitive effects. "The *per se* rule stated in *Schwinn* must be overruled."

Illinois Brick Co. v. *Illinois*, 431 U.S. 720 (1977)

Facts: The state of Illinois and hundreds of local governments brought treble-damage suits under section 4 of the Clayton Act alleging an agreement among several manufacturers to fix the price of concrete block in violation of the antitrust laws. The manufacturers sold the block directly to masonry contractors for use in building masonry structures. Those structures were incorporated into entire buildings that were sold to plaintiffs. They claimed that section 4 provided a remedy to them as indirect buyers of concrete block insofar as the illegal overcharge by the manufacturers was passed on by masonry and general contractors and thereby inflated the price of the buildings. The district court entered judgment for the defendants on the theory that section 4 fails to authorize a treble-damage remedy for indirect purchasers. The court of appeals reversed.

Question: Does section 4 of the Clayton Act authorize indirect purchasers to recover treble damages for an illegal overcharge upon proof that the overcharge was passed on to them through intervening links in the distribution chain?

Decision: No. Opinion by Justice White. Vote: 6–3, Brennan, Marshall, and Blackmun dissenting.

Reasons: In *Hanover Shoe, Inc.* v. *United Shoe Machinery Corp.*, 392 U.S. 481 (1968), the Court held that, except in special circumstances, an antitrust defendant sued for treble damages by a direct purchaser under section 4 may not reduce the amount of recovery by proving that the plaintiff passed on part of its illegal overcharge to indirect purchasers. *Hanover Shoe* refused to permit a passing-on defense for two reasons. First, treble-damage actions would become unmanageably complex if allocation of the effects of an illegal overcharge among all purchasers in the distribution chain were attempted. Second, indirect purchasers ordinarily lack a financial incentive to sue. Thus, a passing-on defense would permit antitrust violators to retain some of the fruits of their illegality. Those reasons dictate the holding in this case.

To permit indirect purchasers to recover under section 4 would inject economic evidence and procedural problems of bewildering complexity into treble-damage actions.

> The evidentiary complexities and uncertainties involved in the defensive use of pass-on against a direct purchaser are multiplied in the offensive use of pass-on by a plaintiff several steps removed from the defendant in the chain of distribution. The demonstration of how much the overcharge was passed on by the first purchaser must be repeated at each point at which price-fixed goods changed hands before they reached the plaintiff.

The invocation of complex procedural rules would be necessary, moreover, if the threat of duplicative recovery were to be avoided and the rights of each claimant in the distribution chain were to be protected.

To permit recovery by indirect purchasers under section 4 would reduce the treble-damage incentives of direct purchasers by raising their litigation costs and lowering their prospective recoveries. This would undermine vigorous private enforcement of the antitrust laws, a major aim of section 4. "We conclude that the legislative purpose in creating a group of 'private attorneys general' to enforce the antitrust laws under section 4 is better served by holding direct purchasers to be injured to the full extent of the overcharge paid by them than by attempting to apportion the overcharge among all that may have absorbed a part of it."

Brunswick Corp. v. *Pueblo Bowl-O-Mat, Inc.*, 429 U.S. 477 (1977)

Facts: An owner of bowling centers brought a treble-damage suit against a large manufacturer of bowling equipment (Brunswick), alleging that the manufacturer had violated the antimerger provisions of section 7 of the Clayton Act.[98] The owner claimed that Brunswick had acquired several bowling centers that had defaulted on loans owed to Brunswick. The theory of the damage claim was that the acquisitions deprived the plaintiff of profits that would have accrued had the competing bowling centers ceased operations. Both the district court and court of appeals held that the Clayton Act authorized a recovery of treble damages under that theory.

Question: Does the Clayton Act authorize an award of treble damages when the sole injury alleged is that an anticompetitive merger resulted in the continuing operation of business competitors, thereby denying the plaintiffs an anticipated increase in market shares?

Decision: No. Opinion by Justice Marshall for a unanimous Court.

Reasons: Section 7 of the act condemns mergers or acquisitions that *may* lessen competition. Section 4 authorizes damages only for *actual* injury to business or property. Accordingly, a section 7 violation permits a recovery of damages only if the plaintiff proves that it in fact caused him injury. In addition, the injury must be linked to the reason why the merger was condemned under section 7. Congress did not intend section 4 to permit damages caused by reasons of no concern to the antitrust laws.

> We therefore hold that for plaintiffs to recover treble damages on account of section 7 violations, they must prove more than injury causally linked to an illegal presence in the market. Plaintiffs must prove *antitrust* injury, which is to say injury of the type the antitrust laws were intended to prevent and that flows from that which makes the defendants' acts unlawful.

Here the questioned acquisition was alleged to be a violation of section 7 because Brunswick, with its enormous size, entered the bowling center market occupied largely by small businesses. But the type of injury alleged—loss of profits that would have been realized if the acquired centers had ceased business—bears no relationship to either the size of the acquiring company or that of its competitors. That so-called loss would have occurred if the acquiring company

---

[98] Under section 4 of the act, any person may recover treble damages for injury to his "business or property" caused by "anything forbidden in the antitrust laws." Section 7 generally prohibits mergers or acquisitions that may substantially lessen competition in any line of commerce in any section of the country.

had been small or if the acquired centers had obtained refinancing. The injury thus lacked a causal relationship to the antitrust policy that allegedly made the Brunswick acquisitions unlawful.

U.S. Steel Corp. v. Fortner Enterprises, Inc., 429 U.S. 610 (1977)

Facts: Fortner Enterprises agreed to purchase prefabricated houses from U.S. Steel on the condition that U.S. Steel finance the cost of acquiring and developing the land on which the houses would be located. After difficulties had been encountered in development of the land, Fortner brought a treble-damage action against U.S. Steel, claiming that it tied the sale of prefabricated houses to the use of its credit in violation of the Sherman Act. In 1969, the Supreme Court reversed a summary judgment against Fortner, holding that a Sherman Act violation could be established upon proof that U.S. Steel possessed "appreciable economic power" in the market for the tying product, credit. On remand, the district court found that U.S. Steel had sufficient economic power in the credit market to make the challenged tying arrangement unlawful. The court of appeals affirmed.

Question: Did U.S. Steel possess sufficient economic power in the credit market to make an agreement tying the sale of its prefabricated homes to the purchase of credit unlawful under the Sherman Act?

Decision: No. Opinion by Justice Stevens. Vote: 9–0.

Reasons: The conclusion that U.S. Steel possessed appreciable economic power in the credit market rested on four strands of evidence: that it was a large corporation; that it made tying arrangements with a significant number of customers; that Fortner was charged a noncompetitive price for the prefabricated homes; and that the credit provided Fortner was unique because it covered 100 percent of the costs to Fortner of land acquisition and development.

Simply because U.S. Steel is large, however, implies nothing about its economic power in the credit market. Likewise, the fact that U.S. Steel gave several buyers credit to finance the purchase of its prefabricated homes does not prove economic power over credit. The corporation's noncompetitive price for prefabricated homes may have been offset by its unusually favorable credit terms, thus making the price for the entire package competitive. Finally, the fact that the credit terms offered by U.S. Steel were unique was of no competitive significance absent proof that it possessed some market power over credit. Since such proof was lacking, the unusual credit terms "prove nothing more than a willingness to provide cheap financing in order to sell expensive houses."

Piper Aircraft Corp. v. *Chris-Craft Industries, Inc.*, 430 U.S. 1 (1977)

Facts: Chris-Craft Industries sought to obtain control of Piper Aircraft through a public exchange offer of Chris-Craft securities for Piper stock. Characterizing the Chris-Craft offer as inadequate, Piper management supported an alternative public offer of Bangor Punta securities for Piper shares made by the Bangor Punta Corporation. While the Bangor Punta offer was pending, Bangor Punta privately purchased 120,000 shares of Piper from three large institutional investors in violation of Rule 10b-6 promulgated pursuant to the Securities Exchange Act. In addition, Bangor Punta filed misleading registration materials with the Securities and Exchange Commission regarding its exchange offer. After a nine-month takeover battle, Bangor Punta held more than 50 percent and Chris-Craft 42 percent of Piper stock.

Chris-Craft then sued Piper management and Bangor Punta in federal district court for damages caused by its unsuccessful tender offer. It claimed the defendants unlawfully blocked its takeover attempt by violating Rule 10b-6 and section 14(e) of the Williams Act. While section 14(e) generally prohibits misleading statements or deceptive practices in connection with any tender offer, it is silent on the question of whether a private right of damages exists for persons injured by its violation. After protracted litigation in both the district court and court of appeals, Chris-Craft was awarded $36 million in damages for the violation by the defendants of section 14(e) and violation by Bangor Punta of Rule 10b-6.

Question: Did Chris-Craft have an implied cause of action for damages under section 14(e) of the Williams Act or under Rule 10b-6 based on alleged antifraud violations committed by Bangor Punta and the Piper management?

Decision: No. Opinion by Chief Justice Burger. Vote: 7–2, Stevens and Brennan dissenting.

Reasons: The Williams Act was adopted primarily to protect stockholders solicited in corporate takeover attempts through the use of tender offers. It requires takeover bidders to file a comprehensive statement with the Securities and Exchange Commission, including such information as the source and amount of funds to be used in making stock purchases and the bidder's plans with regard to the target corporation. Shareholders tendering their stock are guaranteed equitable treatment. In addition, section 14(e) contains a broad antifraud prohibition applicable to persons making, supporting, or opposing tender offers. Against this background, Chris-Craft argues that section 14(e) authorizes a private damage remedy for unsuccessful tender offerors.

In prior cases interpreting antifraud provisions of the Securities Exchange Act, some private rights of action have been implied. But this has occurred only where the statutory purpose of an antifraud statute would likely be undermined absent private enforcement. Here the predominant purpose of the Williams Act was to protect shareholders of the target company, not tender offerors such as Chris-Craft. This was to be achieved in part by ensuring full and accurate disclosure of information by both management and tender offerors in takeover battles. "We find no hint in the legislative history . . . [of the Act] that Congress contemplated a private cause of action for damages by one of several contending offerors against a successful bidder or by a losing contender against the target corporation." To imply a private right of action by defeated tender offerors, moreover, would add little if any protection to target shareholders, the intended beneficiaries of the Williams Act. Chris-Craft, as a defeated tender offeror, thus lacked an implied cause of action for damages under section 14(e).

Likewise, Rule 10b-6 afforded Chris-Craft no private right of action on account of its unsuccessful tender offer. That rule is designed, *inter alia*, to prevent an issuer whose stock is in the process of distribution from tampering with the market by purchasing its own shares. Bangor violated Rule 10b-6 when it purchased Piper stock (and thus the right to buy Bangor stock) while its public tender offer was pending. In these circumstances, however, Rule 10b-6 offered protection to purchasers of Bangor stock who may have paid excessive prices caused by market manipulation, not Chris-Craft who claimed injury only as a defeated tender offeror. Rule 10b-6 affords no remedy for a lost opportunity to obtain control of a corporation.

Santa Fe Industries, Inc. v. *Green,* 430 U.S. 462 (1977)

Facts: Under the Delaware "short-form merger" statute, a parent corporation owning at least 90 percent of the stock of a subsidiary may merge with that subsidiary upon approval of the board of directors of the parent company. The statute does not require notice or consent of minority shareholders, but permits them to demand fair value for their shares as determined by a court-appointed appraiser. Pursuant to the statute, Santa Fe Industries merged with Kirby

Lumber Corporation. Declining to pursue their appraisal remedy, minority stockholders of Kirby brought suit in federal district court seeking to set aside the merger or recover fair value for their shares on the ground that the merger violated Rule 10b-5 promulgated under the Securities Exchange Act of 1934. Rule 10b-5 generally prohibits any scheme or device to defraud a person who either buys or sells a security. The basic theory of the complaint was that Santa Fe had obtained a fraudulently low appraisal of the value of Kirby stock for the purpose of freezing out minority stockholders at an inadequate price. No misrepresentation or nondisclosure was alleged. The district court dismissed the complaint for failure to state a claim. The court of appeals reversed, reasoning that Rule 10b-5 reaches breaches of fiduciary duties owed by the majority to minority stockholders, even when no misrepresentation or lack of disclosure is alleged.

Question: Did the complaint of the minority stockholders state a claim under Rule 10b-5?

Decision: No. Opinion by Justice White. Vote: 8–1, Brennan dissenting.

Reasons: Rule 10b-5 prohibits any "artifice to defraud" or any act "which operates or would operate as a fraud or deceit" in connection with the purchase or sale of a security. This language and the legislative history of its authorizing statute, section 10(b) of the Securities Exchange Act, indicate that it was intended to cover only "deceptive" or "manipulative" securities transactions. The minority stockholders did not allege any deception in the short-form merger. Santa Fe provided truthful information concerning the value of their shares, and the minority was free to seek an appraisal remedy if dissatisfied with the price Santa Fe offered. Manipulation within the meaning of section 10(b) refers to practices, such as wash sales, matched orders, or rigged prices, intended to mislead investors by artificially affecting market activity. The complaint alleged no such manipulation. Dismissal of the complaint is consistent with the general philosophy of the Securities Exchange Act. It was largely designed to serve as a full-disclosure law, not to police fiduciary duties. An appraisal remedy under state law, moreover, was available to the dissatisfied stockholders. Finally, to extend Rule 10b-5 to the type of corporate conduct questioned in this case would overlap and possibly interfere with state corporate law. "Absent a clear indication of congressional intent, we are reluctant to federalize the substantial portion of the law of corporations that deals with transactions in securities, particularly where established state policies of corporate regulation would be overridden."

E.I. Du Pont de Nemours and Co. v. Train, 430 U.S. 112 (1977)

Facts: The Federal Water Pollution Control Act amendments of 1972 authorize the administrator of the Environmental Protection Agency to order various pollution control measures for the purpose of eliminating all discharges of pollutants into U.S. waters by 1985. Section 301 of the act provides that by 1983 "effluent limitations for categories and classes" of point pollutant sources shall require "application of the best available technology economically achievable for such category or class." Interim 1977 effluent limits are to require application of the "best practical control technology currently available." Invoking authority under section 301 and other provisions, the administrator issued regulations, applicable to both new and existing sources of pollutants, which established industrywide effluent limitations for inorganic chemical manufacturing plants for 1977 and 1983. The regulations allowed variances for existing plants, but not for new plants, regarding the 1977 limitations. Eight chemical companies sought review of the regulations in a federal court of appeals, claiming that the administrator was limited to the establishment of effluent limitations on a plant-by-plant basis in connection with the issuance of pollution discharge permits. The court of appeals generally rejected the claim, but held that the administrator was required to establish procedures for new plants to obtain variances from the promulgated discharge limits.

Question: Does the Federal Water Pollution Control Act authorize the administrator of the Environmental Protective Agency to establish industrywide effluent limitations for existing and new sources of pollutants without permitting variances for new plants?

Decision: Yes. Opinion by Justice Stevens. Vote: 8–0. Powell did not participate.

Reasons: Section 301 speaks in terms of setting effluent limitations on "categories and classes" of sources of pollutants. Both legislative history and administrative practicality support the conclusion that section 301 authorizes industrywide effluent limitations. A contrary view would require the administrator "to give individual consideration to the circumstances of each of more than 42,000 dischargers who have applied for permits, and to issue or approve all these permits well in advance of the 1977 deadline in order to give industry time to install the necessary pollution control equipment."

Neither the act nor the regulations expressly contain any variance provision for new sources of pollutants. Relying on its view of appropriate regulatory processes, the court of appeals inferred that the act intended to allow for variances. Unlike variances for existing sources of pollutants, however, there is no statutory provision for new-source variances; to infer such a provision would conflict with the goal of the act in ensuring national uniformity and maximum feasible control of new sources of pollution.

State Taxation and Regulation of Commerce

The commerce clause, the contract clause, due process, the supremacy clause, and federal statutes all circumscribe state power to tax and to regulate commerce. The limits of these restraints were tested in a variety of circumstances this term, as states battled in several cases to extend their taxing and regulatory powers to alleviate fiscal difficulties.

The states won important doctrinal victories in two cases challenging their authority to tax interstate commerce. In one, *National Geographic Society* v. *California Board of Equalization*, 430 U.S. 551 (1977), the Court sustained the imposition of the burden of collecting a use tax on an out-of-state mail order business that lacked any in-state presence tied to the business. Because the parent organization had unrelated in-state contacts that profited from municipal services, the Court reasoned, neither due process nor the commerce clause raised any obstacle to the questioned burden.

The Court discarded a twenty-six-year-old commerce clause barrier to state taxation in *Complete Auto Transit, Inc.* v. *Brady*, 430 U.S. 274 (1977). It overturned the rule of *Spector Motor Service* v. *O'Connor*, 340 U.S. 602 (1951), that prevented states from taxing the privilege of engaging in interstate commerce. Under *Complete Auto Transit*, such privilege taxes pass constitutional muster if they are applied to activities having a substantial nexus with the taxing state, are fairly apportioned and nondiscriminatory, and are fairly related to services offered by the state.

In a third decision upholding the taxing authority of a state, that in *United States* v. *Fresno County*, 429 U.S. 452 (1977), the Court ruled that federal employees could not invoke the shield of the supremacy clause to prevent state taxation of their leasehold interests in federally owned houses.

States were soundly rebuffed in four cases in which they sought to protect local business or extricate themselves from fiscal problems. The most significant was *United States Trust Co. of New York* v. *New Jersey*, 431 U.S. 1 (1977). There the Court resurrected the constitutional contract clause to invalidate an attempt by New York and New Jersey to reduce the security of bonds issued by the bistate port authority. A bond covenant was repealed in order to permit greater subsidies for mass transit operations. In holding the repeal unconstitutional, the Court may have brought financially pressed states and municipalities a blessing in disguise. Similar covenants may be demanded by future bondholders, and state or local officials may willingly acquiesce in order to build a constitutional defense against demands for ever-increasing spending.

The states of New York, North Carolina, and Virginia were all defeated in seeking to shield local business from out-of-state competition. New York structured its transfer tax on securities transactions to favor in-state securities sales by nonresidents. That favoritism, said the Court in *Boston Stock Exchange* v. *State Tax Commission*, 429 U.S. 318 (1977), runs afoul of the commerce clause. North Carolina, lacking any state-graded apples, sought to limit the sale of apples in closed containers to those bearing either a federal grade or no grade at all. As an obstacle to the marketing of Washington State–graded apples carrying state grades equal or superior to federal grades, the Court reasoned in *Hunt* v. *Washington State Apple Advertising Comm'n*, 432 U.S. 333 (1977), the limitation unconstitutionally burdened and discriminated against interstate commerce. Virginia preferred residents over nonresidents and aliens in issuing licenses to fish commercially in its territorial waters. In *Douglas* v. *Seacoast Products, Inc.*, 431 U.S. 265 (1977), the Court held that the preference could not prevail over federal licensing laws that conferred a right to be free from discriminatory state regulation. In another federal pre-emption decision, that in *Jones* v. *Rath Packing Co.*, 430 U.S. 519 (1977), the Court invalidated a state weight-labeling law because it frustrated or added to the demands of comparable federal laws.

Finally, in *Shaffer* v. *Heitner*, 433 U.S. 186 (1977), the Court undercut the authority of states to hale nonresidents into state courts by threatening loss of property located in the state. Delaware sought to compel nonresident officers and directors of a Delaware corporation to answer personally in a lawsuit alleging a breach of their fiduciary duties because of corporate infractions committed out of the state. To induce their appearance in person, a Delaware court sequestered $1.2 million of the defendants' stock having a legal situs in Delaware. Overturning the sequestration, the Supreme Court extended the rule of *International Shoe Co.* v. *Washington*, 326 U.S. 310 (1945), to the exercise of any type of state court jurisdiction: *in personam, quasi in rem,* or *in rem.* Derived from the due process clause, that rule prohibits the exercise of jurisdiction by a state court over a defendant or his property unless he has maintained "minimum contacts" with the state "such that the maintenance of the suit does not offend traditional notions of fair play and substantial justice."

National Geographic Society v. *California Board of Equalization,* 430 U.S. 551 (1977)

Facts: The National Geographic Society, a nonprofit corporation of the District of Columbia, operates a mail-order business that sells maps, atlases, globes, and books. In accord with California statutes, National Geographic was assessed a use-tax collection liability of several thousand dollars for its mail-order sales to California residents. National Geographic maintained two offices in California that solicited advertising for its *National Geographic* magazine, but performed no activity related to its mail-order business. Suing in state court, it sought a tax refund on the theory that the mail-order sales lacked a sufficient nexus to California to justify imposition of the burden of collection of a use tax under either the commerce clause or the due process clause of the Fourteenth Amendment. The California Supreme Court upheld the constitutionality of the tax.

Question: Did imposition by California of a use-tax collection liability on National Geographic violate either the commerce clause or the due process clause?

Decision: No. Opinion by Justice Brennan. Vote: 7–0. Burger and Rehnquist did not participate.

Reasons: Both the commerce clause and the due process clause limit the power of a state to impose the burden of collecting and paying use taxes on out-of-state sellers. The burden survives constitutional attack only if the seller has a "sufficient nexus" to the taxing state. That test is satisfied if the out-of-state seller enjoys substantial services of the taxing state, whether or not the services are related to the sales that trigger the use-tax collection liability.

In this case, National Geographic maintained two California offices that solicited advertising for its magazine, which amounted to approximately $1 million annually. The offices had the benefit of numerous municipal services such as fire and police protection. "The Society's continuous presence in California in offices that solicit advertising for its Magazine provides a sufficient nexus to justify that State's imposition upon the Society of the duty to act as collector of the use tax."

Complete Auto Transit, Inc. v. *Brady,* 430 U.S. 274 (1977)

Facts: Mississippi imposes a tax on the privilege of doing business within the state equal to 5 percent of the gross income derived from intrastate activity. A motor carrier that transports motor vehicles from out-of-state locations to Mississippi dealers challenged the constitutionality of the tax solely on the ground that the commerce clause, Article I, section 8, clause 3, prohibits a state from taxing the privilege of engaging in interstate commerce. It was not alleged that the Mississippi privilege tax discriminated against interstate commerce, was unfairly apportioned, or was unrelated to services provided by the state. The Mississippi Supreme Court upheld the tax.

Question: Does the commerce clause forbid a state from taxing the privilege of doing business within the state when that business consists solely of interstate activity?

Decision: No. Opinion by Justice Blackmun for a unanimous Court.

Reasons: In *Spector Motor Service* v. *O'Connor,* 340 U.S. 602 (1951), the Court held that a state is barred under the commerce clause from taxing the privilege of engaging in interstate activity, irrespective of its practical effects. The commerce clause, however, was not designed to relieve interstate commerce from its just share of state tax burdens, although such burdens increase the cost of doing business. Decisions subsequent to *Spector* have sustained the constitutionality of state taxes on interstate business "when the tax is applied to an activity with a substantial nexus with the taxing state, is fairly apportioned, does not discriminate against interstate commerce, and is fairly related to the services provided by the State." The *Spector* rule "that a state tax on the 'privilege of doing business' is *per se* unconstitutional when it is applied to interstate commerce" lacks any relation to economic realities or the main purposes of the commerce clause, and the *Spector* decision is therefore overruled.

United States v. *Fresno County*, 429 U.S. 452 (1977)

Facts: Employees of the United States Forest Service were provided housing by the federal government in national forests located in Fresno County, California. Although required to occupy the federally owned houses to increase efficiency, the employees paid the Forest Service the fair rental value of their lodgings. Pursuant to California law, Fresno County levied property taxes on the employees' possessory interests in the federally owned houses. Paying under protest, the federal employees sued for a refund in state court claiming that the questioned taxes interfered with the operations of the Forest Service and discriminated against federal employees, in violation of the supremacy clause of the U.S. Constitution. A state appellate court sustained the constitutionality of the taxes.

Question: Was Fresno County constitutionally barred by the supremacy clause from taxing federal employees on their possessory interests in housing owned and supplied to them by the federal government as part of their compensation?

Decision: No. Opinion by Justice White. Vote: 8–1, Stevens dissenting.

Reasons: In *McCulloch* v. *Maryland*, 17 U.S. 316 (1819), the Court established the general doctrine that the federal government enjoys immunity from state taxation under the supremacy clause of Article VI. This immunity extends to taxes imposed directly or whose legal incidence falls on the federal government. Immunity does not automatically attach, however, to nondiscriminatory state taxes that may increase the costs of operations to the federal government. In *City of Detroit* v. *Murray Corp. of America*, 355 U.S. 489 (1958), *United States* v. *City of Detroit*, 355 U.S. 466 (1958), and *United States* v. *Township of Meshegon*, 355 U.S. 484 (1958), the Court upheld state taxes on the use of federally owned machinery and other property leased to private companies for commercial purposes. In two of the cases, the tax fell on companies with cost-plus federal contracts requiring reimbursement for state taxes paid by them. The rule to be derived from this trilogy of decisions "is that the economic burden on a federal function of a state tax imposed on those who deal with the Federal Government does not render the tax unconstitutional so long as the tax is imposed equally on the other similarly situated constituents of the State." The requirement of nondiscrimination creates a political check on the potential abuse of the taxing powers of a state to obstruct federal functions.

In this case, the questioned property tax was not levied directly and its legal incidence did not fall against the federal government or federal property. It was levied solely on private citizens working as federal employees. Insofar as it burdens the Forest Service by decreasing its attractiveness as an employer, the tax must be upheld if it is nondiscriminatory.

The contested tax is imposed only on renters of real property located on tax-exempt land. It seeks to achieve property-tax parity with lessees located on taxable lands whose rents reflect the property taxes paid by the lessors. Consequently, the Forest Service employees "are no worse off under California tax laws than those who work for private employers and rent houses in the private sector." Thus, the Forest Service employees suffered no constitutionally cognizable discrimination in paying the Fresno County property tax.

United States Trust Co. of New York v. *New Jersey*, 431 U.S. 1 (1977)

Facts: The Port Authority of New York and New Jersey was established in 1921 by a bistate compact to improve the transportation and other commercial facilities connected with the port of New York. Supported substantially by bridge-toll revenues and bonds sold to private investors, the Port Authority is authorized to purchase, lease, and operate transportation facilities within its jurisdiction. In 1962, the Port Authority increased its involvement with rail passenger transportation. New Jersey and New York sought to promote continued confidence of investors in Authority bonds by placing a ceiling on mass-transit deficits that it could finance in the future. This was accomplished by the enactment of a statutory convenant in which both states agreed with affected bondholders that revenues or reserves pledged as security for their bonds would not be diverted to pay for mass-transit deficits except under narrowly circumscribed conditions. Thereafter, the Port Authority sold "Consolidated Bonds" to private investors to finance the purchase and operation of a rail passenger system. Faced in 1974 with burgeoning mass-transit deficits and an energy crisis, both New York and New Jersey repealed the 1962 statutory covenant in order to permit the Port Authority to expand its mass-transit operations. The trustee of the Consolidated Bonds brought suit in state court against New Jersey claiming that the repeal of the covenant impaired the contractual obligations of the state to the bondholders in violation of Article I, section 10, clause 2, of the Constitution (the contract clause). The New Jersey Supreme Court sustained the constitutionality of the repeal.

Question: Did the repeal by New Jersey and New York of their 1962 statutory convenant that protected the security given to Port Authority bondholders from impairment caused by mass-transit deficits violate the contract clause of the Constitution?

Decision: Yes. Plurality opinion by Justice Blackmun. Vote: 4–3, Brennan, White, and Marshall dissenting. Stewart and Powell did not participate.

Reasons: The scope of the contract clause must be harmonized with the constitutional recognition of broad police powers possessed by the states. In *Fletcher* v. *Peck*, 10 U.S. 87 (1810), it was established that the contract clause limits the power of states to modify their own contracts with private parties. Here it is not disputed that the repealed 1962 statutory covenant was a contractual obligation of New York and New Jersey to the holders of Consolidated Bonds. Although the reduced value of the bonds attributable to the repeal is uncertain, the repeal did eliminate an important security protection for the bondholders and thus impaired the obligation of the states' contract.

Not all impairments of contractual obligations assumed by a state, however, violate the contract clause. A state legislature lacks power to bargain away the police powers of the state. "The Contract Clause does not require a State to adhere to a contract that surrenders an essential attribute of its sovereignty." While police powers and the power of eminent domain are essential attributes of state sovereignty, the power to assume a purely financial obligation is not. Thus, the 1962 statutory covenant was subject to the restraints of the contract clause.

Those restraints, however, do not bar states from impairing a contractual obligation "if it is reasonable and necessary to serve an important public purpose." The proffered justification for repealing the 1962 covenant was to divert users of private automobiles to mass transit by raising bridge and tunnel tolls and using this additional revenue to subsidize commuter rail service. This justification lacks constitutional merit for two reasons: first, increased mass-transit subsidies could have been obtained through a modification rather than repeal of the covenant; second, the states had numerous alternative means of reducing the use of private automobiles and improving mass transit. The repeal of the 1962 covenant, moreover, was not the product of unforeseen circumstances; the need for mass transit in the New York metropolitan area and the probability that the operation of commuter railroads would produce large deficits were known when the covenant was adopted. Although the severity of these problems increased during the twelve-year period beginning in 1962, "we cannot conclude that the repeal was reasonable in light of changed circumstances."

Boston Stock Exchange v. *New York State Tax Commission*, 429 U.S. 318 (1977)

Facts: New York State amended its transfer tax on securities transactions in 1968 to discourage the sale of securities outside the state. Under the amendment, the transfer tax on nonresidents is reduced by 50 percent if the sale occurs within New York. In addition, the total transfer tax liability of any taxpayer is limited to $350 for any transaction that involves a sale of securities in New York. If the sale occurs without the state, the $350 ceiling is lifted. Several regional stock exchanges brought suit in New York state court claiming that the 1968 amendment unconstitutionally discriminated against interstate commerce by imposing higher taxes on out-of-state, as opposed to in-state, sales of securities. The state court rejected the claim.

Question: Does the 1968 transfer-tax amendment discriminate against interstate commerce in violation of the commerce clause, Article I, section 8, clause 3, of the Constitution?

Decision: Yes. Opinion by Justice White for a unanimous Court.

Reasons: The principal object of the commerce clause was to create an area of free trade among the several states. It operates to limit state power in various ways even without federal legislation. One well-established limitation prohibits a state from discriminating against interstate commerce by providing an advantage to local business. Otherwise, preferential trade areas within states would proliferate and subvert the commerce clause goal of encouraging economically efficient national markets.

The 1968 transfer-tax amendment creates a tax structure that discriminates against the sale of securities outside New York. It offers protection to the securities business of the state by reducing certain taxes on sales within the state. The amendment offends the free-trade goals of the commerce clause, and is thus constitutionally flawed.

STATE TAXATION AND REGULATION OF COMMERCE

The fact that the challenged amendment partially favors local business by discriminating between two different types of interstate commerce—favoring nonresident sales in-state over resident sales out-of-state—does not save it from constitutional condemnation. "A State may no more use discriminatory taxes to assure that nonresidents direct their commerce to businesses within the State than to assure that residents trade only in intrastate commerce." In either case, the purpose or effect conflicts with the free-trade purpose of the commerce clause.

Hunt v. *Washington State Apple Advertising Comm.*, 432 U.S. 333 (1977)

Facts: The state of Washington has an Apple Advertising Commission charged with the statutory duty of promoting and protecting the apple industry of the state. Its members are elected by apple growers and dealers, and its activities are financed entirely by assessments levied upon the apple industry. The commission brought suit in federal district court attacking a North Carolina statute that required apples sold or shipped into the state in closed containers to bear either a U.S. Department of Agriculture grade or no grade at all. For more than sixty years, Washington State has required all domestically produced apples shipped in interstate commerce to be tested and graded under standards that are equal or superior to the comparable federal grades and standards. Thus, the commission claimed, the questioned statute placed an undue and discriminatory burden on the interstate sale of Washington apples in violation of the commerce clause because it prohibited the display of the state's grades and standards for marketing purposes. Concluding that the commission had standing to bring the suit, the federal district court invalidated the statute on the ground that it unconstitutionally discriminated against interstate commerce.

Questions: (1) Did the commission have standing to attack the apple-labeling statute? (2) Does the labeling statute violate the commerce clause of the U.S. Constitution?

Decision: Yes to both questions. Opinion by Chief Justice Burger. Vote: 8–0. Rehnquist did not participate.

Reasons: Past decisions

have recognized that an association has standing to bring suit on behalf of its members when: (a) its members would otherwise have standing to sue in their own right; (b) the interests it seeks to protect are germane to the organization's purpose; and (c) neither the claim asserted, nor the relief requested, requires the participation of individual members in the lawsuit.

Here Washington apple growers and dealers had standing to attack the North Carolina labeling statute. It caused them to either obliterate state grades from preprinted closed containers, abandon the use of such containers, or lose North Carolina accounts. These injuries are sufficiently concrete to make a "case or controversy" constitutionally cognizable by federal courts. In addition, the assertion by the commission of the interests of the growers and dealers was germane to its purpose of promoting the sale of apples. Finally, the challenge to the labeling statute by the commission did not require individualized proofs from growers and dealers. Thus, if the commission were a voluntary membership association, its standing would be clear.

Although the commission is a state agency, its constituency and functions are sufficiently similar to those of traditional trade associations to permit its assertion of the claims of the state apple growers and dealers. The commission has a financial stake in the outcome of the litigation, moreover, because the assessments due from growers and dealers are tied to the volume of apples packaged with the label "Washington State." In these circumstances, it would exalt form over substance to deny the commission standing to assert the rights of individual growers and dealers.

State statutes regulating interstate commerce are constitutional only if they are nondiscriminatory, advance legitimate state interests, and avoid imposing an undue burden on interstate commerce. Here the contested apple-labeling statute discriminated against Washington apple growers and dealers in several ways. First, it raised the costs to them of doing business in North Carolina by forcing alterations in their marketing practices while leaving North Carolina producers unaffected. This is because North Carolina has no state system for grading apples. Second, it destroyed the competitive and economic advantages the Washington apple industry had acquired through a long history of maintaining a reputable inspection and grading system. Third, it required Washington apples of superior grade to be marketed under inferior federal grades, thereby preventing their sale at premium prices.

North Carolina contends that these discriminatory effects were necessary if the statutory purpose of eliminating a multiplicity of confusing and deceptive apple labels was to be achieved. This argument is faulty in two respects. Since the statute permits the marketing of ungraded apples in closed containers, the elimination of deception and confusion cannot fairly be claimed as its major goal. The fact that well-informed apple wholesalers and brokers, not consumers, are the principal purchasers of closed containers of apples fortifies this conclusion. In addition, North Carolina could reduce deception or confusion without discriminatory effects by requiring state-graded apples equal or superior to comparable federal grades to carry labels marked with both grades. If some confusion still persisted, it would be of the type that states must tolerate under the commerce clause.

Douglas v. Seacoast Products, Inc., 431 U.S. 265 (1977)

Facts: Virginia favors residents over nonresidents and aliens in issuing licenses to fish commercially in its territorial waters. Aliens (including corporations that are more than 75 percent owned by aliens) are precluded from obtaining any commercial fishing licenses. Nonresidents are denied the right to obtain licenses to fish for menhaden in the Virginia portion of the Chesapeake Bay. Several corporations owned virtually entirely by aliens and denied fishing licenses under Virginia law brought suit challenging the constitutionality of the law on various theories. The corporations owned fishing vessels enrolled and licensed under federal law. A three-judge federal district court held Virginia's discrimination against aliens and nonresidents unconstitutional.

Question: Are Virginia laws that discriminate against aliens and nonresidents in the issuance of commercial fishing licenses preempted by federal enrollment and licensing laws governing fishing vessels?

Decision: Yes. Opinion by Justice Marshall. Vote: 7–2, Rehnquist and Powell dissenting in part.

Reasons: In fields traditionally occupied by state law, as here, federal pre-emption will be found only if that was the clear and manifest purpose of Congress. In *Gibbons* v. *Ogden*, 22 U.S. 1 (1824), the Court invalidated a state regulation that discriminated against vessels possessing a federal license to engage in the coasting trade. At a minimum, the holding of *Gibbons* was that the federal Enrollment and Licensing Act conferred on federally licensed vessels a right to be free from discriminatory state regulation. Since *Gib-*

bons, Congress has repeatedly reenacted the act in virtually the same form and has thereby ratified the *Gibbons* interpretation.

The discriminatory Virginia licensing laws denied the alien-owned corporations their federally granted right to engage in fishing on the same terms as Virginia residents. They are thus invalid under the supremacy clause, Article VI, clause 2. Provisions of the Submerged Lands Act giving states ownership and broad regulatory powers over lands beneath the ocean and natural resources located in state territorial waters do not undermine this conclusion. That act expressly retained federal powers over these lands and waters for the purpose of regulating commerce. Since the grant of a federal fishing license is made under the commerce power, "the Submerged Lands Act did not alter its pre-emptive effect."

The Court added that its decision would not bar states from enacting "reasonable and evenhanded conservation measures, so essential to the preservation of our vital marine sources of food supply."

Jones v. *Rath Packing Co.*, 430 U.S. 519 (1977)

Facts: California ordered the removal of bacon packaged for sale by Rath Packing Co. because the company had violated a state weight-labeling law. It requires that the average weight of any sample of a commodity offered for sale be identical to the weight stated on the package. Flour packaged by three millers was also ordered removed because of violation of the state labeling law. Rath Packing and the millers responded by obtaining a declaratory judgment in federal district court that the state law was pre-empted by federal laws regulating net weight labeling. The court of appeals affirmed.

Question: Do the federal laws regulating the packing and labeling of bacon and flour pre-empt the California weight-labeling law?

Decision: Yes. Opinion by Justice Marshall. Vote: 7–2, Rehnquist and Stewart dissenting in part.

Reasons: Where, as here, it is claimed that Congress has pre-empted a field traditionally occupied by the states, it will be assumed that the historic police powers of the states were not to be superseded by the federal statute unless that was the clear and manifest purpose of Congress. The packaged bacon at issue is subject to inspection under the federal Wholesome Meat Act. That act and supplementary regulations permit reasonable variations in the actual weight of a meat product and the net weight indicated on the label. The variations are intended to accommodate the reduced weight resulting from loss of moisture during the course of distribution. The act prohibits the imposition of labeling requirements different from those it requires, moreover. The California weight-labeling law, as applied to packaged bacon, was pre-empted for failure to allow the reasonable variations from actual weight that are permitted under federal law.

The Federal Food, Drug, and Cosmetic Act and the Fair Packaging and Labeling Act (FPLA) regulate the net-weight labeling of millers' flour. These statutes and implementing regulations provide for the same weight-labeling standards as those for meat. In addition, a major purpose of the FPLA is to facilitate value comparisons among similar products. This requires that packaged products having the same indicated weight also have the same actual weight. Flour gains or loses moisture after milling is completed depending on the humidity of the atmosphere in which it is stored. Federal law permits variations in stated weight caused by this gain or loss. Packages meeting federal labeling requirements will contain the same amount of flour solids.

California, however, refuses to permit reasonable weight variations resulting from the loss of moisture during distribution. To meet the weight-labeling standard of California a miller must ensure that loss of moisture does not bring the weight of the contents below the stated weight. Local millers could do so by adjusting their packaging practices to the humidity of their region. National manufacturers, in contrast, would be forced to overpack because the destination of their flour at time of packing would be unknown. Thus, as a result of the application of the California standard, consumers comparing the value of identically labeled packages of flour would not be comparing packages with identical amounts of flour solids. This would preclude accurate value comparisons and thus undermine a major objective of the FPLA. Under such circumstances, the supremacy clause of Article VI requires that the state law yield to the federal.

Shaffer v. Heitner, 433 U.S. 186 (1977)

Facts: A stockholder of Greyhound, a Delaware corporation, brought a shareholder's derivative suit in Delaware state court against Greyhound, a wholly owned subsidiary, and twenty-eight present or former officers or directors of the two corporations. The complaint alleged that the defendant officers and directors had breached their corporate duties by causing Greyhound and its subsidiary to undertake conduct in Oregon that violated the antitrust laws and constituted criminal contempt. As authorized by Delaware law, the plaintiff stockholder also obtained an order that sequestered $1.2 million of Greyhound stock owned by the individual defendants for the purpose of compelling their personal appearance.[99] As nonresidents of Delaware, the individual defendants entered a special appearance and unsuccessfully moved to dismiss the derivative suit and to vacate the sequestration order on constitutional due process grounds. They claimed that under the rule of *International Shoe Co. v. Washington*, 326 U.S. 310 (1945), their contacts with Delaware were insufficient to justify jurisdiction of the state court over the pending suit. The Delaware Supreme Court affirmed a judgment upholding jurisdiction of the state court over the individual defendants.

Question: Did constitutional due process bar Delaware state courts from asserting jurisdiction over officers and directors of a Delaware corporation in a stockholder's derivative suit based on out-of-state misconduct?

Decision: Yes. Opinion by Justice Marshall. Vote: 7–1, Brennan dissenting. Rehnquist did not participate.

Reasons: International Shoe established the general due process rule that a state court may exercise *in personam* jurisdiction over a defendant only if he has maintained certain "minimum contacts" with the state "such that the maintenance of the suit does not offend traditional notions of fair play and substantial justice." The derivative suit at issue here, however, was brought as a *quasi in rem* proceeding in which jurisdiction was premised on the technical location of Greyhound stock in Delaware. A judgment in the suit would only affect the ownership of the stock and could not subject the individual defendants to personal liability. But irrespective of whether a state court is asserting *in personam, quasi in rem,* or *in rem* jurisdiction, the claims that it decides will affect substantial rights of persons concerning property or other matters. Thus, all assertions of jurisdiction of a state court should be and are constitutionally limited by the minimum-contacts standard enunciated in *International Shoe.*

Jurisdiction of the Delaware court over the individual defendants in this case is based solely on the technical location of Greyhound stock

---

[99] Failure to enter a personal appearance could lead to a default judgment against the defendants up to the value of the sequestered property.

there. That isolated contact does not satisfy due process because the stock is unrelated to the merits of the suit. Defendants had no other contacts with Delaware sufficient to meet the fair-play and substantial-justice standards of *International Shoe*. The complaint failed to allege that any wrongdoing occurred in Delaware or that the individual defendants ever set foot there. The defendant officers and directors never purposefully availed themselves of the privilege of conducting activities within Delaware, and they lacked any expectation that a breach of corporate fiduciary duties occurring in Oregon might lead to their being haled before a Delaware court. Delaware does not require officers or directors of Delaware corporations to own corporate stock, moreover, or to consent to suit in the state.

Denying Delaware courts jurisdiction over the defendant officers and directors of Greyhound will not undermine the legitimate interest of the state in supervising and regulating the management of Delaware corporations. Under conflict-of-law rules, the law of the state of incorporation is generally held to govern the liabilities of officers or directors to the corporation and its stockholders.

Presidential Papers

In 1974, the landmark decision of the Court in *United States* v. *Nixon*, 418 U.S. 683 (1974), prompted the public disclosure of presidential tape recordings that led to President Nixon's resignation. Shortly thereafter, a depository agreement was concluded between Nixon and the General Services Administration (GSA) to govern the disposition of presidential papers and tape recordings. Fearing the destruction or disappearance of important information, Congress, acting with uncharacteristic haste, nullified the agreement in passing the Presidential Recordings and Materials Preservation Act. Applicable only to President Nixon, the act directs the GSA to assume custody of Nixon's presidential papers and tapes, to separate purely personal and private materials for return to Nixon, and to arrange for public access to the retained materials, subject to specified terms and conditions.

This term, in *Nixon* v. *Administrator of General Services*, 433 U.S. 425 (1977), the Court rebuffed Nixon's initial constitutional challenges to the facial validity of the act. The separation-of-powers doctrine, executive privilege, the rights of privacy and political association, and the bill-of-attainder clause were abortively invoked in the effort by Nixon to capture control over the contested papers and tapes. The Court declined, however, to foreclose future constitutional attacks on the implementation of the act regarding specific papers or tapes. Thus, once the GSA commences to separate and to to disclose matters that it concludes are of public interest, renewed litigation appears likely.

Comparable litigation could be spawned if Congress should heed the final report of the National Study Commission on Records and Documents of Federal Officials. Established by the Presidential Recordings and Materials Preservation Act, the commission has recommended that the official records of congressmen, federal judges, and high-level executive officials should be publicly disclosed under the Freedom of Information Act, with special procedural protections.[100] Each of these officials would be permitted to impose restrictions on access to their public papers for a maximum period of fifteen years after leaving federal service. Thereafter, the papers would be publicly disclosed except where restriction on access might be necessary to protect the national security or to prevent an unwarranted invasion of privacy. The disclosure requirements would not be enforced retroactively.

The public papers of federal judges would consist of documentary materials, exclusive of court records, generated or received by members of the judiciary in connection with their official duties and retained after final judgment in particular cases. Included would be conference notes and bench memoranda prepared by law clerks.

Nixon v. Administrator of General Services, 433 U.S. 425 (1977)

Facts: Shortly after his resignation in August 1974, President Nixon signed a depository agreement with the Administrator of General Services, Arthur Sampson, to govern the disposition of his presidential papers and tape recordings. The Nixon-Sampson agreement provided that 42 million pages of presidential documents would be stored by the United States in an area accessible only through the use of two keys, one of which would be held by Nixon. During the first three years, Nixon agreed not to withdraw any original materials, but thereafter he would have unrestricted access and use. The agreement provided for the storage by the government of 880 tape recordings until September 1, 1979. The administrator agreed to destroy such tapes after that date as Nixon directed; all remaining tapes would be destroyed at the time of Nixon's death or September 1, 1984, whichever occurred first.

---

[100] See *The Third Branch*, July 1977, p. 1.

Fearful that the Nixon-Sampson agreement would result in the destruction of important presidential papers and tapes, Congress passed and President Ford signed the Presidential Recordings and Materials Preservation Act in December 1974. Nullifying the agreement, the act directs the administrator to take custody of Nixon's presidential papers and tapes and to issue regulations providing for the separation of purely personal and private materials for return to Nixon, and the terms and conditions of public access to the retained materials. Before the promulgation of any regulations, Nixon brought suit attacking the constitutionality of the act on the grounds that it violated the separation of powers, executive-privilege doctrines, his rights to privacy and freedom of association, and the bill-of-attainder clause. A three-judge federal district court sustained the facial constitutionality of the act and held that questions regarding public release of materials under yet-to-be-published regulations were not ripe for judicial review.

Question: Is the Presidential Recordings and Materials Preservation Act facially constitutional?

Decision: Yes. Plurality opinion by Justice Brennan. Vote: 7–2, White, Blackmun, and Powell concurring, Burger and Rehnquist dissenting.

Reasons: Separation of powers. A former President may assert a separation-of-powers or executive-privilege claim despite the absence of a dispute between the incumbent President and another branch of government. Nixon claims that the act represents an unconstitutional congressional intrusion into the executive powers of the President by conferring authority to release presidential papers and tapes on a subordinate official of the executive branch. Rejected by both Presidents Ford and Carter, this claim misapprehends the nature of the separation-of-powers doctrine. It does not prescribe a hermetic seal between the three branches of government. It demands only that each branch avoid obstructing another from accomplishing its constitutionally assigned functions. Here the act gives custody of the contested presidential materials to the executive branch. It subordinates use of the materials in judicial proceedings or their public disclosure to any rights or privileges that Nixon or others may have. "[W]hatever are the future possibilities for constitutional conflict in the promulgation of regulations respecting public access to particular documents, nothing contained in the Act renders it unduly disruptive of the Executive Branch and, therefore, unconstitutional on its face."

Executive privilege. United States v. *Nixon,* 418 U.S. 683 (1974), recognized a qualified constitutional privilege of the President to maintain the confidentiality of presidential papers and conversations in order to encourage a candid and uninhibited exchange of views and advice. Although the privilege may be invoked by a former President, the fact that neither President Ford nor President Carter supports the claim would seem to undermine the assertion that the act will chill the free exchange of views in the executive branch.

The act on its face authorizes an insubstantial intrusion on constitutionally protected presidential communications. It provides for the screening of President Nixon's papers and tapes by a few career archivists in the executive branch who have an unblemished record in handling confidential materials. The limited exposure of this group to confidential presidential communications is necessary to permit the separation and return to Nixon of purely personal and private papers and the retention of the remainder for legitimate historical and governmental purposes. In promulgating regulations governing public access to the retained materials, the act directs the administrator to consider "the need to protect any party's opportunity to assert any constitutionally based right or privilege." There are thus strong safeguards against public disclosure of protected communications built into the act, and the screening process is nothing more than a marginal intrusion into the confidentiality of the presidency. In these circumstances, "the claims of presidential privilege clearly must yield to the important congressional purposes of preserving the materials and maintaining access to them for lawful government and historical purposes."

Privacy. The privacy claim rests on the exposure to archivists of Nixon's papers and tapes concerning purely personal and private matters during the screening process. President Nixon does have a legitimate expectation of privacy in such materials, but that expectation erects no constitutional barrier to the limited and reasonably necessary infringement of privacy resulting from the act.

It is conceded that no more than 220,000 out of the 42 million documents and 880 tapes at issue contain purely private matters. Screening is clearly necessary to separate the purely private matters from other materials of legitimate public interest. The exposure of private matters to a few screening archivists constitutes a minimal intrusion on privacy interests. When weighed in the context of President Nixon's status as a public figure, his lack of privacy interests in the overwhelming majority of materials at issue, and the public interest in preserving these papers and tapes, the intrusion on his privacy passes constitutional scrutiny.

Freedom of political association. Records of President Nixon's private and partisan political views are commingled with other presidential papers and tapes covered by the act. The archival screening process needed to separate these records, it is said, will deter persons from expressing political views to Presidents and constitutes punishment for past political activity. As with the privacy claim, however, the exposure of Nixon's constitutionally protected political views will be limited to that necessary for screening. The views are contained in a relatively small number of records, and whatever political chill flows from their limited exposure is outweighed by the important government interests promoted by the act.

Bill-of-attainder clause. Article I, section 9, clause 3, of the Constitution prohibits the enactment of any "Bill of Attainder." A legislative act that inflicts punishment on a named individual or group for the purpose of condemning past behavior violates this prohibition. Under this test, President Nixon's bill-of-attainder claim is faulty for several reasons.

Although the act is expressly limited to President Nixon's papers and tapes, this fact does not automatically render it a bill of attainder. Congress thought it necessary to act hastily because of the Nixon-Sampson agreement. The papers of all former Presidents from Hoover to Johnson were already housed in presidential libraries. The act also calls for a special commission to recommend legislation regarding the records of future presidents. "In short, [President Nixon] constituted a legitimate class of one, and this provides a basis for Congress's decision to proceed with dispatch with respect to his materials while accepting the status of his predecessors' papers and ordering the further consideration of generalized standards to govern his successors."

In addition, the act did not inflict punishment on Nixon. The Court has held that a wide variety of legislative sanctions may constitute punishment under the bill-of-attainder clause, including disqualification from government or professional employment.

Nixon, however, suffers no deprivation of liberty or property under the act, which authorizes the payment of just compensation for presidential papers or tapes that the judiciary determines he owns. The objectives of the act, moreover, were nonpunitive: to guarantee the availability of evidence at criminal trials and to preserve materials of significant historical and legislative interest. Finally, the legislative history of the act evinces no evidence that Congress was punishing Nixon for blameworthy offenses. It scrupulously provides safeguards to protect his opportunity to assert constitutional rights to block the public release of presidential documents or tapes.

> We . . . are not blind to [President Nixon's] plea that we recognize the social and political realities of 1974. It was a period of political turbulence unprecedented in our history. But this Court is not free to invalidate acts of Congress based upon inferences that we may be asked to draw from our personalized reading of the contemporary scene or recent history.

INDEX OF CASES

SUBJECT INDEX